Praise for *Simply*... **EMPOWERED!**

*"Crystal Andrus has overcome a personal story that would leave
many feeling victimized and small. She has not only risen to become a
dynamic, passionate, and empowered woman, she has carefully crafted
a how-to manual for the rest of us to follow! If you are ready
to become the hero of your own life, this book will get you there!*
Simply . . . EMPOWERED! *is one of this year's <u>must-reads</u>!"*

— **Debbie Ford,**
the #1 *New York Times* best-selling author of
The Dark Side of the Light Chasers

*"***Simply . . . EMPOWERED!*** *is the total package.
A complete guide to creating the life of your dreams.
Practical, inspiring, and accessible,* **Simply . . . EMPOWERED!**
is simply wonderful!"

— **Christiane Northrup, M.D.,**
the *New York Times* best-selling author of *Women's Bodies,
Women's Wisdom* and *The Secret Pleasures of Menopause*

"If you are serious about personal growth, then **Simply . . .
EMPOWERED!** *is for you! Crystal Andrus has an honest,
no-nonsense, straightforward approach that can absolutely liberate
you. Step by careful step, question by question, and self-appraisal
survey followed by yet another all gently lead the reader from one
simple self-discovery to an ultimate epiphany. In my opinion, whether
you seek a change in your body image, your personal relationships,
your success patterns, or any other aspect of your personal life, this is
'a must' manual for accomplishing a genuine breakthrough!"*

— **Eldon Taylor,**
the *New York Times* best-selling author of
Choices and Illusions and *Mind Programming*

Simply...
EMPOWERED!

Simply...
EMPOWERED!

Discover How to CREATE and SUSTAIN
Success in Every Area
of Your Life

CRYSTAL ANDRUS

HAY HOUSE, INC.

Carlsbad, California • New York City
London • Sydney • Johannesburg
Vancouver • Hong Kong • New Delhi

Published and distributed in the United States by: Hay House, Inc.: www
.hayhouse.com • *Published and distributed in Australia by:* Hay House
Australia Pty. Ltd.: www.hayhouse.com.au • *Published and distributed
in the United Kingdom by:* Hay House UK, Ltd.: www.hayhouse.co.uk •
Published and distributed in the Republic of South Africa by: Hay House
SA (Pty), Ltd.: www.hayhouse.co.za • *Distributed in Canada by:* Raincoast:
www.raincoast.com • *Published in India by:* Hay House Publishers India:
www.hayhouse.co.in

Design: Charles McStravick

Library of Congress Cataloging-in-Publication Data

Andrus, Crystal.
  Simply-- empowered! : discover how to create and sustain success in every area
of your life / Crystal Andrus. -- 1st ed.
      p. cm.
  ISBN 978-1-4019-2654-0 (tradepaper : alk. paper) 1. Success. 2. Self-realization
in women. 3. Women--Psychology. 4. Women--Health and hygiene. I. Title.
  BF637.S8A524 2010
  158--dc22

2009037571

ISBN: 978-1-4019-2654-0

13 12 11 10   4 3 2 1
1st edition, March 2010

Printed in the United States of America

This book
is dedicated to my CREATOR–
who taught me how to
CREATE!

CONTENTS

PART II: SUSTAIN

PREFACE

I woke up the other night at three in the morning to a voice, or perhaps it was more like a feeling, nudging me to pick up my journal and pen. I listened. The following words poured out of me . . .

"Do you really believe you have to prove your worth to me? Do you not know that I know your worth?

"I think that you think I've given you your success and can take it away.

"Crystal, you created your success. You did your part. It was effortless for me to do mine. Always has been. You are the creator of your destiny. And only you, Crystal, can take away your dreams, hopes, future, and accomplishments. Not I! Besides, why would I take it away?

"Stop fearing. You will always be okay because you now know that you can always create success. You understand what it takes to create, and finally, you've learned the secret of how to sustain.

"So create! Not to show me your worth and not to prove yourself to anyone, but because it is what you want. It is your self-written destiny, and you are simply remembering your own plan. Remember, I only want for you what <u>you</u> *want!*

And I will always do what I can to help guide and support you.

"Think about it: If Madelaine [my daughter] wants to be a movie star because that is what lifts her up and makes her feel alive, wouldn't you want that for her? Isn't that unconditional love?

"And if she achieves it by working hard, staying focused, and being in the right place at the right time, would you take it away from her—even if she does something to upset you or let you down? (By the way, you cannot take away her success nor can I take yours. I gave you free will, and I will never take it away!)

"If Julia [my other daughter] wants to be a rock star, wouldn't you help her if you could? And if she is doing everything she can possibly do, and you can help guide her to the right people, and support and encourage her, wouldn't you?

"On the other hand, if Julia begs and pleads with you every day to make her a rock star, but she lies around, meditates on it, cries about it when it doesn't happen, fears that it will never happen, complains that it's happening for other less-talented, less-deserving people, gets focused and then loses focus weekly (sometimes daily) . . . would there really be anything you could do to fulfill her dreams?

"Do you see the dilemma I so often face? Can you imagine my children thinking I've forsaken them? That I won't give them what they desire and dream of? That I won't help them?

"If only they would realize that I've given them the greatest gift of all: free will, free choice, and the ability to take action; as well as my unconditional love, support, guidance, and encouragement!

"Creation is about <u>action</u> and sustaining is about <u>reaction.</u>

"How do you react when you don't get what you want? How do you react when you don't like what you see?

"If only my children could see that their life is a culmination of their actions and reactions, they would understand that success is their creation.

"What power and strength they would feel! What success they would create! What a life they would sustain!"

INTRODUCTION

$\mathcal{W}$e all want success. Everyone desires a body, health, income, relationship, home, career, sensuality, and spirituality that they love. We all want to feel empowered, strong, and inspired. We all want to experience abundance, joy, and love. Some of us achieve it (or at least part of it), while others endure one letdown after another. Yet very few of us can actually create a magnificent life and sustain it. It's almost as if we've been programmed to believe that what goes up must come down. Just as our lives are beginning to take shape, we're already gearing up for the inevitable fall.

I've been there—feeling on top of the world *and* at the bottom. I've felt indestructible at times and broken at others. I've experienced great love and lost it . . . a booming career, then bottomed out. I've felt "holier than thou" and then ashamed of my actions. I've had confidence coming out my "yin yang" only to feel defeated, insecure, and unsure within a few short years. I've felt ugly, fat, thin, beautiful, old, young, scared, and completely and utterly content.

I always thought it was normal—just part of the human condition.

The rise and fall.

Predictable. Unavoidable.

In fact, I've always believed in "the higher the high, the harder the crash," but I was up for it. The highs were too good to live without! I was wrong, though, and just didn't know any better. I was simply living what I'd been taught and "re-creating my future" based on past experiences. It was all I knew, but now I know better. And I'm about to show you that, although tough times are a part of life, it's not what happens to you but what you do with what happens that sets your life in motion; the road ahead has nothing to do with the road just traveled. It's new terrain.

I've discovered that you're not who you've been—you are the potential of who you'll become, and you can become anyone you choose to be. You are the co-creator of your destiny . . . the captain of your ship. Whether you realize it or not, your actions (or lack of action) and reactions will either blow you out into the stormy seas of life or guide you toward the most wonderful adventures you could ever dream of. The choice is yours. I'm just here to help you navigate.

To guide you along the journey, I've created acronyms for the words *create* and *sustain* (see the Contents), and I guarantee that if you follow them, you'll live a long, successful, empowered life! You'll soon see that the majority of this book is dedicated to Part I: "Create." Just like pushing a huge boulder uphill, creation takes far more effort than sustaining something, yet sadly, most people *can't* keep up the success they've created because they aren't ready—that is, *they don't have the simple but necessary tools to sustain their goals.* They even unwittingly sabotage their efforts. Once momentum is on your side, however, you can sustain success by following some basic principles as outlined in Part II: "Sustain."

And when you've moved into the "sustaining part," should you make a bad choice or should something beyond your control spiral you downward, don't worry. You simply need to go back to the beginning—return to the first chapter and *clean it up*. Besides, you'll move through the steps faster the second time around. (The average American millionaire has gone bankrupt or out of business three and a half times! Subsequent failures are most likely due to bad habits that haven't been cleaned up!)

What you'll soon find out is that sustaining success doesn't mean you won't ever experience the repercussions of a bad choice again—no matter how it occurred. It means that you will, naturally, go back to Step 1 and clean up whatever mess has occurred, and then move on to Step 2—*reinventing, rewriting, reprogramming, and rebuilding* your future. This system will eventually become second nature as you effortlessly move back to a position of empowerment.

Hopefully you'll realize, sooner than later, that *all* of creation is governed by a very fragile balance; in order for that creation to take hold—to grow and sustain—it depends on the reactionary factors. Those who have figured out how to maintain this delicate balance understand the yin and yang that regulates life. Just like different types of plants require different care (where some need more nitrogen in the soil or more sun and water to grow), individuals have a different balance that allows them to blossom. This means that your life—your success—isn't about you doing things the way someone else does them . . . or the way someone else thinks that you should do things! It's about *you* learning what works *for you*. It is *you* discovering what lights *you up* and having the courage and integrity to live it, *even if no one else gets it!*

I've also shared many of my own personal stories here—not to impress you or imply that you should be like me, but rather to impress upon you that each of us has tales of woe and wonder. Sometimes it's through sharing our struggles and triumphs that we can put our lives in perspective and become authentic, accepting, and truly empowered people!

I'd love to read *your* story! Please send it to **crystal@crystal andrus.com**, and we may share it on our Website at **www .crystalandrus.com** to inspire others.

Here's to making all of your dreams come true!

Love,

Crystal Andrus

PART I

Create

❖ ❖ ❖ ❖ ❖ ❖ ❖ ❖ ❖

Chapter One

CLEAN IT UP

"Staying busy exhausts us.
Holding on keeps us stuck. Avoiding 'what is' robs us.
Running away disempowers us. Our saving grace is that our
consciousness will continue to show us what must be cleaned up
in order for us to heal, evolve, create, and sustain."

— *Crystal Andrus*

*W*hen it comes to creating an amazing life, most of us just want to get on with it and get to the good stuff. We're ready to get down to business. We want to forget the past and move on. Let bygones be bygones. We're embarrassed about, or ashamed of, certain parts of our lives. What's the point of looking back?

And yet, inevitably, similar to a very long anchor that gets dropped overboard as we're sailing down that wonderful river of life, something always happens that keeps us stuck right where we were. Why can't we keep our raft going downstream? Why are we replaying the same story over and over? *We thought we'd dealt with this!* Or worse, why are we replaying the same story with just a different person or scenario?

Well, until you've truly cleaned things up, they will keep cropping up!

Until you face your past, your not-so-wise choices, and your debtors and demons; and until you confront the reality of what you've fed your body and how you've starved your soul or shrouded yourself in shame, you can continue to avoid the truth, but you can't hide—at least not from yourself! Your guilt and fear will eat away at your ability (and, eventually, even your desire) to succeed; they'll rob you of your power and keep you struggling in the dark. Playing it small will become normal, and you'll never realize your potential.

Self-sabotage is a clear sign that you have something weighing on your conscience. Repress your feelings—your embarrassment, blame, sorrow, sadness, anger, or jealousy—in whatever way you've learned, and they'll find a way to reappear. As long as you try to resist uncovering "it," dealing with it, or healing it, *it* will persist. The burden of carrying it, whether or not you're aware of it, will exhaust you. Weight gain, financial messes, health problems, addictions, disorganization, and relationship woes are ways in which repressed thoughts, feelings, fears, and unmet needs manifest themselves in your outer world.

If you can't seem to create or sustain success, you clearly have unfinished business that must be cleaned up first! Only *you* can clean up your own stuff—even if you think it would be better for someone who's bigger, stronger, richer, or smarter to step in and save you!

What I promise you is that once you clean things up (no matter how hard it may seem), you can take the next step in creating an incredible life! Unfinished business drains your energy and robs you of strength and integrity.

It Is What It Is

Most of us have a hard time seeing the truth about our own lives: the truth about ourselves, our situation, choices, fears, and motivators. We have a hard time accepting that we've created the circumstances we're in—that life *is* what *we* make it!

So if things aren't so great in your life, you must ask yourself, *Why would I create this?* Whether or not you choose to see it, the answer is always there: *It is what it is.*

Are you willing to face the truth and shine a light on "what is," without any judgment, excuses, justification, shame, blame, guilt, or regret? If so—if you're ready to take a peek at things—you're ready to begin the process of creating a magnificent life. If not—if you'd rather choose to deny accountability or not face yourself— then this book isn't for you . . . at least not right now.

Cleaning up your life takes courage. It takes honesty and hard work, and you must be prepared to face the music. It can feel tough at times, but so illuminating at others. It all starts with stepping outside of yourself, almost like an observer, and letting your life be your mirror . . . your truth . . . your gift.

Why not look at your life today but with one catch: Imagine that you didn't know the person staring back at you. Try it. Stand before a full-length mirror and describe the person you see. What would you think of her? What would your reflection tell you about her? Would you see someone who takes care of herself? Someone who eats well, exercises, and honors her temple? Would you see someone smiling, happy, confident, and self-assured? What do her eyes say? Her skin? Nails? Hair? Teeth? Clothing? Weight? Posture? How does she talk to herself when she's all alone?

Now imagine you're a fly on the wall in her home. How does she speak to her family—spouse, children, parents, and/or siblings? How do they treat her? Does she thrive on stress, always creating drama and complications? Or does she speak her truth, even if the people around her don't always agree with her views? Does she keep secrets, preferring to handle things (or at least some things) alone? Or does she live her life like an open book?

Does she spend beautiful quality time with those she loves most? Does she hug, kiss, and say "I love you" often? How does she talk about her friends when they aren't around? Her mate? Parents? In-laws? Children? Is she as honest in person? Is she honest at all?

How is her sex life? Is she passionate and uninhibited or uptight and boring?

Does she constantly think about her past, reliving old fights and hurtful comments? Has she forgiven those who've hurt her, or does she bring things up whenever she needs justification or quick retaliation?

Is her home harmonious, loving, and light? Is her bedroom a beautiful, sexy, feminine sanctuary? Is her bathroom a mini spa retreat? Are there soothing candles, soft music, and wonderful bath products to caress her skin? On the other hand, is her kitchen cluttered, her freezer stuffed with old food, her closet crammed with clothes, and her basement filled with stuff from 15 years ago?

Does she have a poverty-hoarding mentality, or does she trust in the flow of life, spending and saving?

The truth?

What about her income, debt, and long-term planning? Does she know her worth, and does she receive it? Is she financially independent? Does she live within her means? Has she planned for the future while enjoying the present? Is she afraid or excited?

Look at her work. Is it fulfilling, purpose driven, and satisfying? Does it light her up? What does it say about her? Is it balanced with play?

Examine her health. How does she eat? Does she smoke, drink excessively, or take drugs? What's her cholesterol ratio? Her blood pressure? Resting heart rate? BMI? Does she even know the answers to these questions? Does she take responsibility for her well-being, or is she expecting her doctors to fix her when things fall apart? Perhaps she's so much in denial that she doesn't even believe anything will ever fall apart, even though she's neglecting her health?

Review her habits and hobbies. (And not the version she's been sugarcoating.) *The truth!* Does she eat too much, drink too much, shop too much, or gossip too much? Does she waste time on mindless Internet sites or spend money carelessly? Or does she read great books, listen to motivational CDs, journal her feelings, and take action on her plans and dreams? Is she in denial, squandering her most precious commodity—time—or is she clear, sharp, focused, and inspired?

Look deep into her heart. Do you see trust, acceptance, love, and forgiveness, or frustration, anger, animosity, and regret? Do you see long-term true-blue friendships and an honest and deeply committed passionate relationship; or do you see a few fair-weather friends, a lack of intimacy, fear, longing, and loneliness?

What does her reflection say about you?

This is your life. She is you.

Let her life be your mirror. It will show you the truth if you'll allow it. You can keep pretending that it's going to magically get better, but it won't.

❖ ❖ ❖

This exercise isn't intended to shame, blame, or judge you, nor is it meant to make you beat up on yourself. (You probably already do a lot of that!) The purpose is to pull you out of denial and into the reality you've created. You cannot change that which you are unwilling to face. The truth will set you free!

The simple fact remains: You can run as far as you like but whenever and wherever you stop, you'll discover that you're still with yourself—your story, your shame, your guilt, your blame. And no one can save you from that!

"Shh! No One Knows . . ."

Okay, so maybe your boss has no idea that your two-week absence last month wasn't really because you had mononucleosis, maybe your husband doesn't suspect that your late nights at the office aren't really to finish an overdue work project, or your business partner has no idea that you've been secretly hiding money. It doesn't really matter—not when it comes to creating and sustaining an amazing life. Maybe no one else knows but you . . . and that's enough!

Whenever you lack the courage to be honest in your life, you rob yourself of your own dignity, success, and integrity. You unconsciously disempower yourself.

The truth is that we all know that insurance companies stick it to us, banks hit us up with ridiculous fees and hidden costs, and the government overtaxes us; but when we're manipulating one area of our life for the sake of another (and think we're outsmarting everyone—including the Universe), we're setting ourselves up for complications, drama, and a whole bunch of bad karma. *(And you wonder why you can't sustain success?!)*

Just like the saying "What goes around, comes around," the loose ends in your life will eventually unravel. Besides, the secrets don't ever have to be found out—your own fear, guilt, and shame will sabotage you!

Face the Music

We all have things we've held on to for far too long, such as:

◆ Sad stories from our childhood

◆ Bitterness from a relationship gone bad

◆ Anger at someone who has hurt us

◆ Disappointment of a failed business

◆ Shame from lies we've told

◆ Guilt for promises we've broken

◆ Humiliation of being fired or dumped

◆ Toxins from too many parties, too many pills, or too many pizzas

◆ Regret of the "should've been," "could've been," and "ought to have been"

◆ Total overwhelm from collecting too much junk in the garage

Whether it's money you've borrowed but never paid back, a mess that's piling up in your basement, sorrow stuffed away in your heart, or impurities clogging your body . . . until you clean up the mess you've been collecting, consciously or unconsciously, you can never build something strong, safe, solid, and sustainable. You'll have a hard time trusting anyone because you can't even trust yourself! Just look at how many times you've let yourself down. Look at how often you've let others down.

Facing yourself is the most important first step you must take. Trying to dodge this will land you right back to your starting place (here, eventually). When your mind, heart, body, and/or home are filled with self-defeating, self-limiting, toxic baggage, there isn't room for magic to manifest. It's like trying to plant a garden with the most magnificent flowers in a bed of weeds, rocks, and depleted soil. No matter how gorgeous the blooms are or how much you want them to flourish, if you don't clean up the mess that's already there, you can't (no matter how much you wish, want, or visualize a great garden) create it.

It reminds me of the Disney movie *The Lion King*. Do you remember the popular song that the two little drifters taught Simba, the lion king? It was called "Hakuna Matata," meaning "no worries." For a while, the three friends try to put the past behind them, but eventually, Simba's Great Spirit (the voice of his father) urges him to *remember who he is*. He realizes his destiny and knows that he must go home, face the mess he left behind, and take his rightful place in the world.

We are all Simba. We all have a destiny, a rightful place in this world.

Maybe you've felt scared and even ashamed, unsure, and unworthy of your destiny. And now you too are just trying to move on and put the past behind you. But don't the worries always follow you? Doesn't the shame eventually wrap around your ankles, whispering in your ear that your life will never be better because you aren't? Hasn't the pressure of trying to do enough so that you'll feel like you're enough exhausted you? Don't you often find yourself feeling stuck, unsure of where to go or what to do, replaying the past, wishing things had gone differently?

Of course you do . . . if you haven't cleaned things up. *Hakuna Matata!*

The Circle of Life

Imagine a wooden cart with four wheels, the spokes all the same length. As it rolls down a hill, can you see it picking up massive momentum as it moves effortlessly toward the bottom, gently clearing the rocks and small mounds along the way?

Now imagine another wooden cart beside it. Its wheels have different-sized spokes. Some are half a foot long, others are four feet, while a few are only a couple of inches long. A pretty pitiful cart! Can you picture how rocky that ride would be? It would be fairly predictable to say that this cart might flip over halfway down the hill, or at least, it would get there much more slowly than the other one.

Not only is your life similar to a wheel—like a circle with birth, life, and death—it rolls much like a wagon, so much more smoothly when you take the time to clean up all the areas of your life, making your spokes balanced! The larger the wheels, the better the chance you have to coast over any small obstacles that might be in the way.

If your body is filled with impurities, your mind burdened with worry and frustration, your spirit numbed in a dead-end job or toxic relationship, your heart filled with anger or sorrow, or your home cluttered with mess, your circle of life will feel just like that second wooden cart—a complicated and bumpy ride.

So what's off-kilter in your life? Are your spokes different lengths?

Let's divide the areas of your life into a few different categories, and then together, we'll begin to face them, one by one:

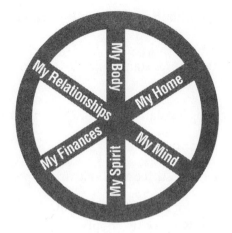

After you've looked at your life through the lenses of an objective observer, you need to write down all the things that need cleaning up. I'm not asking you to tackle them all today, but you do need to get very clear with yourself. You simply can't rewrite your future and sustain success if you aren't honest about everything.

The Circle-of-Life Assessment

Read the statements in each of the six categories of your Circle-of-Life wheel. If the statement is *true,* check the box. At the end of each category, count up the number of check marks.

MY BODY

(Check only those that *consistently* apply to you.)

❑ I get seven to eight hours of uninterrupted sleep each night in a dark room.

❑ I drink eight to ten glasses of pure water per day.

❏ I perform a minimum of 20 minutes of cardio exercise daily.

❏ I do some type of resistance exercise three times per week.

❏ I have orgasms regularly! *(Surprised you, didn't I?)*

❏ My blood pressure is good.

❏ I drink fewer than three alcoholic drinks per week.

❏ If I drive or sit for long periods of time, I stop and stretch my body every two hours.

❏ I don't drink soda.

❏ I rarely consume caffeine (coffee, tea, chocolate, or soda).

❏ I eat only organic foods—primarily fresh fruits and vegetables.

❏ I have comfortable and natural bowel movements daily.

❏ I go for massages, facials, chiropractic adjustments, and/or other alternative-health and spa treatments.

❏ I clean my skin before bed.

❏ I eat fish two to three times a week.

❏ I meditate.

❏ I rarely have mood swings or angry outbursts.

❏ I use a steam bath or sauna a few times per month.

❏ I cleanse my body at a cellular level yearly.

❏ I express my anger in a healthy way.

❏ I bathe in Epsom salts or relax in a hot tub a few times a week.

❏ I cry when my feelings have been deeply hurt.

❏ I have never smoked.

❏ I don't eat red meat.

❏ I rarely eat fast food.

❏ I avoid anything containing hydrogenated or trans fat.

❏ I don't take any drugs.

❏ I rarely eat "white" carbohydrates—such as white bread, rice, pasta, and so on.

❏ I am comfortable in the skin I'm in.

❏ I eat breakfast within one hour of rising every day.

❏ I take omega-3 fish-oil capsules daily.

❏ I eat primarily raw fruits, vegetables, nuts, and seeds.

❏ I limit my use of the cell phone.

❏ I floss daily.

❏ I limit my sodium intake to less than 2,000 mg per day.

❏ I rarely watch television.

❏ My weight is in the ideal range and rarely fluctuates.

❏ I rarely get indigestion.

❏ My cholesterol is at a healthy range.

❏ I have a yearly physical examination with my doctor.

❏ I take daily supplements, including a multivitamin/ mineral.

❏ I consume 60 to 120 grams of lean protein per day.

❏ I have my eyes checked yearly.

❏ I have my teeth cleaned every six months.

❏ My hair is healthy and looks good.

❏ I avoid "acidic" foods such as cheese, meat, white bread, coffee, sugar, alcohol, and so forth.

❏ My nails (fingers and toes) are healthy and clean.

❏ I take weekends off and relax.

❏ I rarely eat sweets or foods containing sugar.

❏ I am very connected with my body and can intuitively feel when something is "off."

TOTAL CHECKED = _____

❖ ❖ ❖

MY HOME (and Physical Environment)

(Check only those that *consistently* apply to you.)

❏ I love my home.

❏ My home is my safe haven and sanctuary.

❏ The energy in my home is light and loving.

❏ My kitchen is clean and organized.

❑ My refrigerator is filled with fresh fruits and vegetables.

❑ I purge my closets every two years.

❑ I have enough space to live comfortably.

❑ My desk is clean and organized.

❑ I light candles or sit by a fire daily.

❑ I keep fresh flowers in my home.

❑ My personal files, papers, and receipts are neatly filed away.

❑ My car is in excellent condition and needs no mechanical work or repairs.

❑ My computer runs efficiently.

❑ I back up my files monthly.

❑ I surround myself with music.

❑ My bedroom is clean, organized, and reflects my personality.

❑ My bathroom has a dimmer switch.

❑ My dining room has a dimmer switch.

❑ My garage is tidy (or shed, basement, or storage space, if you don't have a garage).

❑ I put out the garbage and recycle weekly.

❑ I have a well-kept garden that I tend to myself.

❑ My animals are healthy and well taken care of.

❑ I have many real plants in my home.

❑ My plants are watered.

❑ I have a sacred space somewhere in my home where I meditate, journal, or paint.

❑ My car is clean.

❑ My bed is made daily.

❑ My clothes are clean and pressed before I wear them.

❑ I have no excessive junk, magazines, boxes, or clutter anywhere in the house, including the basement.

❑ I burn incense or pure essential oils.

❑ All of my floors are vacuumed and/or washed weekly.

❑ My home reflects me.

❑ People comment that they like my home and feel comfortable in it.

❑ My grass looks beautiful in the summer, and the driveway is clear in the winter.

❑ I can easily find anything when I need it.

❑ I have a spot for all my office supplies and rarely run out of necessities.

❑ I never run out of toilet paper or paper towels.

❑ My medicine is neatly organized in a discreet place. I never keep anything past its expiration date.

❑ I have my carpets cleaned yearly.

❑ My house has great curb appeal.

❑ I use green products to clean my home.

❑ I use energy-saving lightbulbs.

❏ I compost.

❏ I recycle.

❏ I love to decorate and enjoy making my home look beautiful.

❏ I put away after I use. I pick up after I take off. I close after I open.

❏ I have a well-organized and well-equipped tool box.

❏ I open my windows often to let in fresh air.

❏ I have my furnace cleaned yearly and replace my filters regularly.

❏ *Home sweet home* is my mantra.

TOTAL CHECKED = _____

❖ ❖ ❖

MY MIND

(Check only those that *consistently* apply to you.)

❏ I am conscious of the negative voice in my head.

❏ I understand that my thoughts create my beliefs, and my beliefs create my reality.

❏ I am aware that there is no such thing as truth, but rather my perception of the truth.

❏ I never berate or belittle myself.

❏ I hardly ever watch television.

❑ I rarely self-sabotage.

❑ I am always in the present moment.

❑ I rarely worry.

❑ I read daily.

❑ I am determined and consistent.

❑ I always finish what I start.

❑ I journal daily.

❑ I stop myself when I begin to replay an argument or negative experience in my mind.

❑ I am able to dialogue with the negative voice in my head, and can silence it easily.

❑ I visualize my success.

❑ In my mind's eye, I can see where I want to be 20 years from now.

❑ I write out my seven essential action steps each morning, and I complete them before the day is done.

❑ I rarely focus on problems. I am solution oriented.

❑ I immediately stop myself from reacting when I feel triggered.

❑ I can walk away and assess a situation before reacting.

❑ I am never controlling.

❑ I see a wonderful person when I look in the mirror.

❑ My mind is clear and sharp.

❑ I have no habits that are unacceptable to me.

❏ I grew up with parents who were great role models.

❏ I recite positive affirmations daily.

❏ I remember people's names easily.

❏ I focus on the best in others.

❏ I focus on the best in me.

❏ I focus on finding positive solutions.

❏ I read uplifting books that add to my life force.

❏ I believe I can do anything I put my mind to.

❏ I rarely feel overwhelmed or unfocused.

❏ I take omega-3 EFAs (essential fatty acids) daily.

❏ I rarely get headaches.

❏ I listen well.

❏ I cooperate with others.

❏ I never use self-defeating language.

❏ I only speak positively about others.

❏ I have an excellent vocabulary.

❏ I am well understood.

❏ I heard loving, supportive, and healthy messages while growing up.

❏ I listen before I speak, and I rarely interrupt others.

❏ My mother (if you're a woman) or my father (if you're a man) had no *real* emotional "baggage."

❏ I play word games.

❏   I have a great memory.

❏   I am aware of my choice of words.

❏   I rarely assume the worst.

❏   I say I'm wrong, easily—and mean it.

❏   I felt lovable, special, talented, attractive, and popular while growing up.

TOTAL CHECKED = _____

❖ ❖ ❖

MY SPIRIT

(Check only those that *consistently* apply to you.)

❏   I listen to my instincts.

❏   I trust in myself to take care of myself, *always.*

❏   I never lie.

❏   I am courageous.

❏   I am completely accountable for my life and blame no one for my shortcomings.

❏   I laugh easily.

❏   I smile all the time.

❏   While growing up, my parents urged me to speak my mind, follow my heart, and trust my instincts.

❏   I appreciate the small things in life, such as a sunset, the smell of freshly cut grass, and a bird singing.

❑ I love music.

❑ I dance.

❑ I speak my truth, even if no one else gets it or likes it.

❑ I honor my body.

❑ I honor my needs.

❑ I believe in God or something greater than myself, and I connect with *it* often.

❑ I dream, and I usually remember my dreams.

❑ I trust others.

❑ I see the world as essentially good.

❑ I live my life on my terms.

❑ I have my own sense of style.

❑ When I see a piece of clothing, I immediately know if it's "me."

❑ I know I'm divine.

❑ I know that everyone is divine . . . or everyone has divinity within them.

❑ I embrace life as a wonderfully exciting adventure.

❑ I grew up feeling loved unconditionally.

❑ I am a risk taker.

❑ I am bold.

❑ I am beautiful.

❑ I am smart.

❏ I know I am connected to a divine, universal, collective energy.

❏ I am talented.

❏ I am empowered.

❏ I am unstoppable.

❏ I am clear.

❏ I surrender the things I cannot control.

❏ I am self-aware.

❏ I pray.

❏ I usually make up my mind easily and rarely give it a second thought once a decision is made.

❏ I ask for help when I need it.

❏ I surround myself with beautiful things, kind people, and nurturing surroundings.

❏ I will get the help I need if I feel overwhelmed or unsure.

❏ I respect others' time.

❏ I say no graciously.

❏ I paint, draw, play music, or write.

❏ I see the big picture.

❏ I breathe.

❏ I can relax my body easily.

❏ I sleep well.

❏ I love my body.

❏   I treat all others, including animals, with dignity and respect.

TOTAL CHECKED = _____

❖ ❖ ❖

MY FINANCES

(Check only those that *consistently* apply to you.)

❏   I rarely worry about money.

❏   I know my total monthly expenses, and I live within my means.

❏   I save at least 10 percent of my income.

❏   I pay my bills on time.

❏   My credit rating is excellent.

❏   My parents' credit rating is excellent.

❏   I don't stay awake at night worrying about business or finances.

❏   I've always paid back any money I've borrowed.

❏   I never buy something that I can't afford.

❏   I am honest with myself about my spending habits.

❏   I am honest with my partner/spouse about my spending habits.

❏   Money problems weren't an issue in my home while growing up.

❏ I feel successful.

❏ I am a risk taker and will take educated chances.

❏ I feel authentic when it comes to my financial situation.

❏ I love my career.

❏ I never hide money.

❏ I pay my taxes yearly.

❏ I have six months' living expenses saved in an easily accessible account.

❏ I have a will that is current.

❏ I have life insurance.

❏ I keep all my receipts, and they are organized.

❏ I don't trade my time for money. I've found ways to make passive income.

❏ I feel excited about my future.

❏ I have a one- and five-year financial plan.

❏ My parents taught me healthy messages surrounding money.

❏ I do not have a poverty mentality.

❏ I'm comfortable making large sums of money.

❏ I never "plead poor" or pretend to have less money than I actually have.

❏ I sometimes "fake it till I make it," but I never put myself in financial stress in order to fake it!

❏ I face everything and don't let things fester.

❏ I make an excellent income.

❏ I don't buy lottery tickets. My life is a winning lottery ticket!

❏ I have no unfinished business.

❏ I can easily answer the phone without fear of creditors.

❏ I have no legal cloud(s) hanging over me.

❏ I have a financial advisor whom I meet with biannually.

❏ I have an excellent work ethic and rarely miss work.

❏ I wake up excited about what I do.

❏ I have properly insured all my assets, including my home, car, jewelry, and so forth.

❏ I know when my different bills are due, and I update my checkbook daily.

❏ I never manipulate dealings to make extra money.

❏ I don't have a sense of entitlement to my parents'/siblings'/in-laws' money.

❏ No one has ever called me cheap.

❏ I don't buy love and affection with gifts.

❏ I donate monthly to a charity.

❏ I have a good relationship with my bank manager.

❏ I max out my government-allowed contributions.

❏ I don't bury my head in the sand and hope things

will get better. I take action every day to strengthen my financial situation.

❏ I feel financially empowered.

TOTAL CHECKED = _____

❖ ❖ ❖

MY RELATIONSHIPS

(Check only those that *consistently* apply to you.)

❏ I value relationships more than I value money or assets.

❏ The most important thing in life is the love I've given and received.

❏ I am rarely lonely, even when I'm alone.

❏ I have recently told my parents that I love them—and I mean it.

❏ I have a close relationship with my siblings.

❏ I am in a loving, committed relationship.

❏ I can tell my partner (if in a relationship) absolutely anything, and I never change who I am when I'm with him or her.

❏ I am emotionally stable.

❏ I am honest about my own needs.

❏ I have a best friend whom I trust with my life.

- ❏ I have forgiven everyone who has hurt me.

- ❏ I have asked for forgiveness from anyone I can ever remember hurting.

- ❏ I never play games when I meet someone new.

- ❏ I am a person of my word.

- ❏ I am not easily offended.

- ❏ I do not gossip.

- ❏ I get along well with my co-workers/boss.

- ❏ I have no "burned bridges" in business or pleasure.

- ❏ I am over all of my ex-lovers and have had closure with each relationship.

- ❏ I believe in love.

- ❏ I believe that men/women can be trusted.

- ❏ I forgive myself for any of my past "mistakes."

- ❏ I am trustworthy.

- ❏ I love my life, with or without a lover.

- ❏ I will always help others but not at the sake of myself—my needs or sanctity.

- ❏ I am not a martyr. I don't make decisions from a place of guilt or fear.

- ❏ I accept things I can't control.

- ❏ I notice good things in almost everyone.

- ❏ If I don't click with individuals, I accept it and don't try to win them over.

❑ I am easy to get along with.

❑ I don't expect another person to fulfill me. I fulfill myself.

❑ I am passionate.

❑ I can detach my personal feelings and not "own" someone else's "stuff."

❑ When I make love, I am uninhibited, open, and giving.

❑ I don't put excessive emotional strain on my mate, children, or friends.

❑ I hug my children and tell them that I love them many times a day.

❑ I have never been unfaithful to my spouse, nor has he (or she) been unfaithful to me.

❑ I accept people as they are and feel quite accepted by others.

❑ I rarely feel emotionally triggered.

❑ I have no baggage.

❑ I like who I am, and people tend to like me.

❑ I compromise.

❑ I fight fairly.

❑ I focus on finding solutions rather than on the problem.

❑ I am not needy.

❑ I seek to resolve arguments and carry no grudges.

❏ I pick my battles carefully, but I will "battle" if it is absolutely necessary.

❏ I love sex and enjoy it often.

❏ I love intimacy.

❏ I have no difficulties achieving an orgasm.

TOTAL CHECKED = _____

Each category has 50 questions. Total up each section and place your scores on your own Circle-of-Life wheel. How well would your wagon roll?

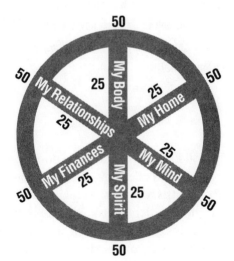

Ask for Help

If the idea of cleansing your body, facing your finances, or silencing your negative mind chatter feels overwhelming, don't hesitate to ask for help. You aren't a master at this yet; don't expect to know how to do it all alone. Feel free to visit me at **www.crystalandrus.com**. In addition, I offer a life-changing 12-Week Body-Mind-Soul Total Transformation TeleCourse that will help you with all of these things, along with a 21-Day Sustain Success Course. Plus, my company has the most amazing "dream team" of coaches: a psychologist specializing in relationships and anxiety, a financial planner and money expert, nutritionists, a spiritualist, an exercise physiologist, cleansing coaches, fitness trainers, a top marathon runner, a personal chef, a teacher, and a life-balancing expert, as well as me. And we all work synergistically to coach you into your power, and you never even have to leave your home! *That's right! When you hire one of us, you get all of us—right over the phone!*

Where to Begin?

At least now you know what has to be done! Remember that you don't have to tackle it all today—besides, you couldn't. But over the next six months to a year, you will have to clean up all the areas of your life in order to sustain success. If you can do it faster, great! But always remind yourself that you aren't fooling anyone by sweeping things under the carpet. You'll only have to deal with the rotting mess that's under there, eventually. Face it now!

The first thing to know is that you may think your money problems are about money or your struggles with your weight are about food—they aren't! I'll explain what's really going on in the coming chapters, but don't jump ahead and try to take shortcuts. That's what's gotten you into any mess you're in now! Don't worry—very soon you're going to be in a whole new place. This week, start with your body and then move toward cleaning up your home—*even if it's your finances or your love life that you're trying to fix!*

Beginning with your body, remind yourself that "cleanliness is next to godliness." Purge your body of all the impurities you've ingested. Do a cleanse! Get yourself strong and stable. Fill your lungs with life-giving oxygen. Exercise! Get your hormones and mood swings balanced. Eliminate sugar, and take fish oils every day! Flush your cells with the fountain of youth. Drink water! Reduce your biological age up to 20 years by limiting alcohol, taking supplements, getting plenty of sleep, meditating, and eliminating red meat and pork. You must begin with a strong physical foundation—a clean body and home.

Next, make sure your safe haven is organized and clutter free. Purge your kitchen of junk, clean out your closets, donate your unused things to charity, light some candles, buy some fresh flowers, and give your walls a fresh coat of paint!

Once you clean up your personal space, you'll have so much freed-up energy to tackle the bigger and really stressful things: your mind, finances, and love life!

The mind is the trickster. It can manipulate you into believing a ton of fallacies. It can rob you of your self-esteem and create delusions and even neuroses! It tells you that you're inadequate and convinces you that if you just buy more things or do more things, you'll be happier. It whispers into your ear that you're flawed and broken as you replay the patterns of your past over and over again, wondering why you can't sustain success. This is probably the place where you've failed before, or perhaps it's what you've tried to skip over. Who has time for this emotional stuff? And then you wonder why you can't maintain financial success or find the love of your life. *You simply can't sustain success without cleaning up your self-defeating and self-limiting messages.*

Once we silence our mind and allow it to do the job it was intended to do (to be the navigational tool for this "vessel" of ours—

the body), we can ignite our spirit and let "it" guide our ship!

With our true master back in charge, we can focus better and face our finances—clean up the mess and make amends, which allows us to create abundance and enter into fulfilling relationships that add to our life force.

You'll effortlessly know what *really* lights you up (this is your spirit), and you'll easily recognize why you let your finances or weight get out of control and/or why you've been stuck in a pattern of dysfunctional relationships. Soon your soul supporters will become easily recognizable, as you speak your truth with dignity, grace, and diplomacy. You'll take action when needed. You'll live and let live. You'll love your life. You'll feel strong, safe, excited, confident, and steady. Your energy will become so magnificent! You'll create relationships based on love, respect, trust, and commitment. You'll feel completely empowered, knowing that rough waters may come along but, with all that baggage gone, you'll feel light, agile, and ready to set sail!

For now, get honest with yourself! Start with your body and home. The rest will unfold in time!

Chapter Two

REINVENT, REWRITE REPROGRAM, AND REBUILD

*"And the day came when the risk
it took to remain tight inside the bud was more painful
than the risk it took to blossom."*

— Anaïs Nin

*W*hen I first began to write this chapter, I nearly changed the title to "Remembering Yourself." Remembering yourself before you felt lost, before you needed to reinvent yourself. Remembering the story you wrote way back before the world told you that who you were and what you wanted were wrong. Way before you created the persona of the person you thought you should be and the life you should have.

Maybe none of this makes sense to you. Maybe you actually believe you really *are* yourself—that your life isn't some kind of story. Do you believe you're living your truth? Maybe you trust the negative voice in your head that puts you down, assumes the worst, and insists on being right. Perhaps you think that life really begins 20 pounds from now, $20,000 from now, or 20 years from now.

It doesn't. But maybe it's been your story for so long that it's hard not to believe it!

Life begins right now.

❖ ❖ ❖

Before you can "Execute Your Plan" (Chapter 3) and rebuild your future, you know that you must clean up anything that has been weighing on your conscience—like it or not. Then you need to recognize what plan—or story— you've been following. *Whether you realize it or not, you've been following a plan. It just might not have been very well organized!*

Your Story

Do you know what your story has been? Do you know what your motivators and discouragers are? Do you know what you hide behind or convince others of so they'll give you what you want? Do you know what you'd do anything to avoid and everything to obtain? Do you know what you believe about yourself, your body, intelligence, capabilities, strength, sexiness, kindness, worthiness, initiative, and sustainability? Do you know what you believe about men, women, parents, children, animals, love, money, sex, God, and power?

You may think you do . . . you may think you don't.

I'm going to tell you that you *do* know, but only if you've done the mirror exercise in Chapter 1. *That's right!* Your life will reflect everything you believe, telling you word for word the autobiography you've been writing. It will reveal what you believe about yourself, along with all of your other beliefs.

If you believe in love, your life will mirror back to you a person who is in love. You may say that you want love, are ready for love, and even that you "love" love; but I'll tell you that if you aren't in love right now, no matter what you think, you *don't* believe! Your mind doesn't believe you're ready . . . yet. Perhaps your mind doesn't trust love. And now part of your story is that you're "someone who isn't good when it comes to love."

If you, on the other hand, have faith that you're able to lose weight, look great, and be healthy, when you look into the mirror, you'll see a person who's fit and attractive, and who exercises and eats well. You may say that you want to lose weight, but if you aren't fit, something in your mind doesn't believe you can do it or doesn't want you to do it. Maybe it has seen "thin and beautiful" as being dangerous or selfish. All the wanting in the world won't change your circumstances. You may be able to create change, but you won't be able to sustain it! Your story is probably more along the lines of "losing weight is harder for me" (due to some reason) or "all the women in my family struggle with their weight—it's genetic!"

All of your stories are based on the things you believe—*not the truth, mind you.* (Now you know why it wasn't about the diets you've tried or opportunities that turned sour. It was about *you!* You sabotaged them.)

If you believe you are smart, capable, and able to make large amounts of money, your bank account will reveal that, too. The only way to know what you believe is to look at your present circumstances without judgment. It will tell you everything . . . believe it or not!

How is your story working for you?

The only way to change your life (or parts of your life) is to change your mind about certain things. If you change your story, you change what you believe. Everyone has heard the saying "I'll believe it when I see it." However, you'll never "see" it unless you first start believing it. You need to reprogram your mind—your software—to believe it. This is the next crucial step in creating an empowered life.

The Trickster

Let's begin by understanding our mind and how it has tried to keep us safe; how it has made decisions based on its perceptions—its beliefs—and not necessarily the truth.

Here's how this happened: You took in all kinds of messages while growing up, and at a certain age (as young as two or three or as old as nine or ten), you began to realize that you couldn't just be yourself because being "just you" was getting you into trouble—or worse, getting you neglected! You started to notice how certain behaviors would result in you being reprimanded or scolded, while others would yield praise and love. You'd rather have some attention than none at all, so your smart little mind began "helping" you, and before you knew it, you had created a new friend—a "voice" in your mind that talked to you all the time, also known as the trickster.

Now don't go thinking you're crazy or that you have a multiple personality. Everyone has a voice they talk to (usually when they're all alone) and that talks back to them (in their mind). *You know the one . . .* when you're getting ready to go out and you hear "the voice" that evaluates how you look or tells you that *it* is offended (and you should be, too) after you leave your mother-in-law's house. It's the "voice" that tells you that you talk too much (or not enough) whenever you go out, or maybe your "voice" tells you that everyone else is better than you are, and you're just not quite good enough.

(*Note:* You might not even realize it's a voice; maybe it has taken over to the point that you're unable to decipher it from the real you.)

At first your voice—or your trickster—occasionally whispered in your ear, but as you grew (and continued to doubt yourself) *its* voice got louder and more regular. It continued to remind you of your "flaws," while giving you what it thought was the best advice to hide them. It has told you exactly what not to be like and what to be like, how to act and how not to act. Your trickster is afraid, and you've spent your life listening to its fears—trying to hide yourself behind your protective masks.

There is a great saying: "What you fear will appear." Have your greatest fears manifested in your outer world yet? If not, they will eventually . . . unless you do this work!

Understanding the Trickster

First things first: The trickster isn't "bad," at least not intentionally. It resonates in a reactive, primordial place—the lowest level of consciousness. It doesn't realize that there's a more empowered way of doing things. Your mind doesn't have to be a trickster, though. It just *is* for most people—for those who haven't done this work yet.

Your mind functions like the hard drive on your computer. When you've downloaded the latest software (including antivirus protection), deleted the stored temporary files and cookies, and defragmented your system, it will run effectively and efficiently. But if you've downloaded corrupt files, stored temporary files and cookies, and failed to optimize your system, your perfectly good computer won't work properly. No matter what you try, if you don't fix the glitches in the operating system, it will continue to run ineffectively.

Imagine how many people are unsuccessfully trying to create magnificent lives that have easily fixable "hiccups" in their hard drives! Remember that once you understand what's going on in your mind, you can address the problems and begin to clean them up in the same way you'd fix your computer.

A great way to imagine how you created your trickster—and how your trickster has taken over—is to compare it to the 1931 movie *Frankenstein.* I'll refresh your memory if you've forgotten or haven't seen this classic film:

Dr. Henry Frankenstein, a zealous young scientist, is consumed with a desire to create human life. He and his devoted assistant Fritz piece together a human body, stitched and sewn from parts that have been secretly collected from various places. Through an assortment of electrical devices that are hooked up to the monstrous, lifeless body, along with an awesome bolt of lightning, the hand of Frankenstein's "monster" begins to move. The excited Dr. Frankenstein cries out: "It's alive!"

The monster slowly rises. It seems he isn't an evil beast at all. In fact, he appears to be a simple, innocent (albeit scary-looking) creature. The doctor greets him and asks him to sit, which he does quite timidly. Fritz, however, comes in with a fiery torch that frightens the monster. His fright is mistaken by Dr. Frankenstein and Fritz as an attempt to attack them, so the monster is beaten and taken to the cellar where he's chained and further antagonized by Fritz and his flame.

The movie carries on with the monster, afraid and confused, escaping from the cellar, then unknowingly perpetrating unspeakable crimes upon the people of the small town—crimes he truly doesn't realize he's committing. He's just reacting in his primitive, instinctive way.

The townspeople, including Fritz and Frankenstein, hunt the monster down, planning to destroy him (thus, the saying: "Be careful what you wish for"). In the end, the monster kills his own creator, Dr. Frankenstein.

In the book *Frankenstein,* written by Mary Shelley, she writes: "The companions of our childhood always possess a certain power over our minds, which hardly any later friend can obtain." The monster, although appearing to be a large half-human man, is merely a child, learning and responding to the world he's in. The monster is like your ego. "He" doesn't know that there's another world out there—a spiritual, empowered, loving place. He doesn't mean to destroy your confidence and self-esteem, your relationships and finances, your health and happiness—he just doesn't know any better! The monster is within you . . . *believe it or not!*

Are You Sure It's Safe to Come Out?

Science has proven that our beliefs, once programmed into our subconscious mind, control our biology for the rest of our lives . . . unless we can figure out a way to reprogram them. So let's just reprogram them! *Right?*

Wrong! It's not quite that simple.

Your mind won't allow you to reprogram your beliefs if it doesn't think that your new beliefs are safe and beneficial. You mind controls your actions. It's like an automatic keyboard that's typing "your story" without you even consciously realizing it! It will direct you to avoid anything it perceives as painful (based on your history) and will urge you to pursue anything it senses as advantageous (again, based on the past). It would have to be safe to create and sustain success. It would have to feel acceptable to reinvent yourself.

So ask yourself: *Do I really feel safe in coming out? Do I really believe that everyone will love me if I change? Will it be okay if I do it differently? Will I be accepted? Will I be too embarrassed or ashamed to admit to my mistakes? Will <u>they</u> be okay if I succeed?*

What do you really believe? Remember that your life will show it to you. Until you debunk these inaccurate and self-limiting beliefs, no amount of wishing or wanting will change things!

The Masks We Wear

I think many extremely successful people are that way because of a need to prove that they were "enough." Deep down, their beliefs (because of messages they heard and saw while growing up) were most likely things such as: "I'm not popular enough, smart enough, thin enough, rich enough, good enough, sexy enough, or lovable enough"; or something along those lines. Their drive in life was to do anything and everything in order to create a world that would feel safe, protected, and successful—*good enough!*

I know this because *I* am one of those people . . .

❖ ❖ ❖

While growing up, I learned that you should always try to be more than you are because who you are, all by yourself, isn't quite enough. I believed that once people were perfect, then they were enough. They were worthy.

I believed that good little girls went to heaven (thus, bad ones went to hell), sex should be saved for marriage, drinking and dancing were sins, good-looking people got attention (and I wasn't good looking), my mother was perfect, and my father was her prince.

I believed that money was the root of all evil but that it also bought power; I believed that power was potent, yet it also intimidated me. I believed that women made less money than men (and were less), that children should be seen but not heard, and that little girls were sugar and spice and everything nice (and should never ever act like Nellie Oleson from *Little House on the Prairie*).

I believed that God loved me, but I needed to prove my worthiness to him—getting into heaven was no easy task! I was taught that marriage was for life, women should make their husbands the "king of the castle," and children were "dirty little rascals." I also knew that a woman's hair was her "crowning glory"; and we should never let our husbands see us without makeup, with curlers in our hair, or in flannel pajamas.

I believed all of these things. I was taught them.

But I also believed I was smart and special.

My parents split up when I was 12, and everything I believed about them and life became skewed. I'd just started attending a school for gifted children at the time and kept my shameful secret from everyone, while trying hard to keep up with all the other "perfect" students.

My wealthy, hardworking father moved in with his new girlfriend—a short, voluptuous, dark-haired woman who was a waitress from the local fish-and-chips restaurant. My gorgeous, fair-haired, *Charlie's Angels* mother was devastated. Once the initial grieving passed, the anger kicked in. She began to work fulltime—*excessive time*—at a local gym, exercising like crazy and partying just as hard afterward. Her new 24-year-old bodybuilder boyfriend, who was a part-time nudist, moved in a few months after Dad moved out. His "specially secluded" times of full-frontal exposure were only when Mom wasn't home or was sleeping. It was the worst in the mornings when he'd cook breakfast naked. The kitchen was beside the front door, and many days I'd miss my bus as I waited in horror until I could execute my escape plan. He particularly loved to take baths with my four-year-old sister, although he never gave up trying to entice me to join him as well. He'd explain to me that the human body was an art form, and I just needed to relax and not be so uptight.

After many months of turmoil, I worked up enough courage to tell my mom. Initially, she was shocked, but after talking with him, she didn't seem to worry. She told me that she asked him to stop, but he never did. Eventually, she asked me to "just not talk about it." Although I pretty much stopped speaking to her altogether, I never became desensitized to *him*. I'd never seen my own father get undressed, so this new form of "art" was just a little too difficult for me to accept. The odd times when he'd French kiss me or touch me in an uncomfortable way would leave me shaking inside and wanting to vomit. I didn't bother telling anyone. He could be pretty nice the rest of the time, and Mom was too busy exercising.

My brother went to live with my dad. My little sister and I couldn't bear the thought of betraying our mother and siding with *the other woman,* but staying at home was becoming a harder option. I'd gone from Sunday school and family dinners to a mother I barely recognized (and rarely saw), a naked "artist" who became our full-time parent, and occasional visits with my father (although we never got to visit him without his girlfriend also being there).

She hated my mom and would constantly point out how much I looked like my (*hiss*) mother. Eventually, she became the cookie-cutter image of my mom—just not quite as pretty. My dad's girlfriend was never happy, though, and she started swigging vodka (straight from the bottle) to help her feel better. I was told that "whatever went on at dad's house stayed at dad's house." I knew that meant I'd better not share the crazy behavior of his new blonde, thin Barbie doll, who insisted on wearing stilettos, huge fur coats, long red nails, and provocative lingerie everywhere, which was especially embarrassing when she'd drop by my school. I still wonder what kind of long-term emotional damage she inflicted on my little sister, Tiffany. God knows that Mom's boyfriend was doing enough harm!

But I believed that if I could be good enough, kind enough, sweet enough, smart enough, something enough . . . someone would see that I was still special.

Someone did think I was special—the man with whom I was sent to live (a relative of my mother's boyfriend). My mom and her new young man had moved into a one-bedroom apartment while they were building their dream house, and they didn't have room for me or my sister. Tiffany was dumped off at Dad's, along with a garbage bag filled with her clothes. I was shipped off to this relative's house and would babysit his children; in exchange, he and his wife would take care of me. Initially, I was relieved. I was so sick of the nudist and thought that this new home would offer some temporary relief . . . unfortunately, though, that's not the way it worked out.

The first time *it* happened I was terrified. The second, third, and fourth times left me feeling sick and dirty. I didn't speak for a week afterward. I had no one to talk to. (Their home was out in the country—it was the summer holiday, and I had no friends.) Over the course of many months, I actually, ashamedly, began to crave the attention. He would come in night after night. I hated what was happening, but for the first time in my life, someone wanted me. I knew it was wrong. I told him it was wrong, but he just said that he loved me and insisted that when I got older, he'd leave his wife and marry me. I couldn't imagine it. I didn't want it! I didn't want *him*.

My own guilt and shame—my trickster—told me that I was a slut and a home wrecker. *He* told me that I was too pretty and too hard to refuse. It wasn't his fault; he was merely a man. He just wanted to make sure that I was never hurt by the boys at school—he wanted sex to be "a wonderful thing" so that I wouldn't be "frigid like his wife." Ironically, during my first year of high school, I was raped by a guy who was five years older than I was. Sex became an unhealthy thing for me—something that seemed to destroy everything. Yet it also seemed to motivate everyone . . . well, men, that is. At the time, this is what I believed.

I felt completely worthless, but I also discovered that I wielded a strange but potent power. My abuser, a man nearly 20 years my senior, became obsessed with me. Boys at school were enamored of me. I got attention everywhere I went *except* from the people who mattered the most to me: my father, mother, brother, and sister . . . my family.

Looking back, it never occurred to me then that I'd been abused—that I was a victim. I believed that I had somehow asked for it. I couldn't imagine facing God now. I was used goods, no longer a virgin. I was a whore. No one needed or wanted me, *except men.*

At 15, I moved out on my own. I was an angry little spitfire. Something in me had woken up, and I was no longer sad. I was mad! I remember the day I ended the "relationship" with my abuser. Pointing at him, I told him that he'd "get his" and that one day his wife would leave him. He vowed she had no idea about us, and I replied that there was never any "us" and that it didn't matter if his wife found out or not—he knew what he had done. God knew. His own guilt would destroy him. His own shame would ruin him. His wife left him one year later. I never told her what had happened, but I wonder how she couldn't have known.

My next relationship was with a man seven years older than I was. As soon as I turned 16, he pursued me until I gave in. I was never really that interested, but I was lonely and he often provided me with food and shelter. As time passed, I acknowledged the fact that I could end up pregnant. (I have no idea why this never occurred to me while I was with my abuser!)

I went by myself to my family physician where I had my first physical and learned about birth control. A few days later, my doctor called to tell me that I had "irregular cell formation" on my cervix, or "cervical dysplasia." I never asked any questions. I'd learned over the years to pretend to understand things, even when I didn't. I kept my mouth shut and found out what I needed on my own. It seemed easier that way; ignorance is often bliss—in the moment, anyway.

Through my own research, I discovered that girls who'd begun having sex at a very young age were more susceptible to this condition, which represented the initial stages of cervical cancer. Taking the city bus by myself to the hospital, I began treatment immediately—embarrassed, scared, and silent. I prayed that no one would ask me when I'd started having sex. If they did, I'd have to lie. The doctor who was treating me kindly offered up the explanation that *it* was often caused by a sexually transmitted virus called human papillomavirus (HPV). Could he tell how many times I'd had sex? Did *I* look like someone with an STD?! His reason (although highly plausible) mortified me even more. Imagine if I had a sexually transmitted virus! I, Crystal Andrus, who had planned on being a virgin until I got married, might have a sexually transmitted virus that was causing cervical cancer! I couldn't remember my doctor saying anything about my having a virus, but I didn't really remember anything he'd said. It was a quick conversation, and I was nervous and afraid. I certainly wasn't going to call him back and ask if I had an STD! For God's sake, I had the initial stages of *cancer*. In my mind, I couldn't figure out which was worse—dying of cancer at 16 or burning in the flames of hell for not being a virgin.

I finally told my boyfriend about my hospital visits—after being accused of sneaking off without telling him where I was. He wanted to know how *it* happened. I, stupidly, told him that it could have been caused from a virus. He was infuriated and became extremely obsessive and jealous. I'd certainly never been unfaithful, but I couldn't dream of sharing the truth— that I was a whore and a home wrecker. Now I was positive that I'd asked for it . . . *all of it*. God was punishing me.

Before long, my boyfriend became physically abusive, too. This time, I fought back and I left him.

On my own, living in a small room with my "fridge," a cooler filled with ice, I became strong beyond my years. I rarely heard from my parents and had never received any financial support; however, I didn't allow myself to focus on that. I vowed that I'd never allow myself to be used or abused again. I was smart. I was focused. I was driven. I was going to prove to the world, to my parents, and maybe *really* to myself that I was special . . . somebody worth loving. During this period, I continued receiving treatments at the hospital, and after 12 months of unsuccessfully trying to freeze the cells into submission, I started a new procedure that burned the cells instead. For more than two years, I'd regularly take the bus to the hospital, all alone. I never asked for help; besides, no one else cared—at least that was the story I was growing to believe.

For a while, my new "strong" mask worked—at least in the ways the outside world viewed as successful. By the time I was 18, I'd moved 21 times. I held down two jobs and was given a partial scholarship to attend a top university. I didn't go at the time, though—I was too interested in making money!

By 19, I bought my first home and moved my 12-year-old sister in with me. She was hitting her teens and, with struggles similar to what I went through, she was desperate for a safe place to live. Raising a teenager when you're still one yourself isn't the easiest thing to do, but I knew I could do it. I'd learned that *if it was meant to be, it was up to me!*

At 21 years of age, I opened my first health club. I competed in international fitness shows (funny how I fell into the same "world" as my mother; perhaps I was still desperate for her approval). I worked hard to look perfect, act perfect, and do everything perfectly in order to hide my shameful past. But deep down, I never felt good enough, no matter what I achieved. For goodness' sake, my own parents didn't even want me! My mom never bothered with any of *my* shows, still too consumed with her own life. Finally, after coming home from competing in the Ms. Galaxy pageant (a week of strutting around in a bikini), I'd decided that I'd had enough. To me, it was all so demeaning and pointless. I was smart. I wanted more. I wanted love and to feel special! To the world, I looked happy, beautiful, and very successful, but I was getting tired. I knew that I was too young to feel so exhausted . . . so empty . . . so sad.

That's when I decided that marriage and children would "fix" me. *Babies would certainly make me feel loved!* I was sure of it. Don't all kids love their mom? It took no time to choose a mate. My boyfriend and I had been living together for a few years, and I easily convinced him that we needed to get married. For about two days, we considered having a wedding, but then my mother told me she wouldn't come if my dad was there, so eloping just seemed like an easier option. Who cared, *really?* I didn't even bother getting a proper wedding gown. When we came home from our "honeymoon," no one wanted to watch our matrimonial video. I guess our family didn't view our marriage as real. It was becoming very clear that my family would never care about me or my life.

But I'd learned that anything else I wanted, I got. I wanted to be married, and I got it. I realized that anything I did, I did well; whatever I touched turned to gold. And so it was natural and expected that I'd get pregnant immediately. It took two months to conceive.

Becoming a mother was about being the "best mother," and that meant being totally immersed in my children. My marriage and life were going to be idyllic—I was going to be everything my parents weren't. I gave up my booming career and moved my family out of the city to a gorgeous house on the water in a small picturesque town. I cooked, cleaned, and poured myself into this new life. I wasn't going to be superficial and shallow. I had everything. I was happy for a while, but 80 pounds and two babies later, it all caught up with me.

My judging voice—the one that had constantly belittled me and compared me to others—had finally won. It told me that I was playing it safe and being a good little woman. I'd created a life that was out of harm's way: I lived in the country and had eliminated any free-spirited friends and all of my male friends. (They only reminded me of my own guilt and shame.) I'd squashed any dream or goal that might take me away from home, even for just an overnight business trip. I had no one to help me—not even a babysitter. I'd convinced myself that women who left their babies and husband obviously didn't love them the way I did. *I* was willing to forsake myself and my dreams for my children—in fact, I was happy to do it. *I* was a good woman. *It was a small sacrifice!*

Soon my husband, who was once attentive, sweet, and scared of losing me, became a serious bodybuilder, obsessed with looking good and making money. (What you fear, you draw near! *Ha!*) When the police banged down our door early one morning with a search warrant charging him with "conspiracy to traffic anabolic steroids," I knew my glass castle was shattering.

Thank God my spirit woke me up so young! I was finally starting to realize that my mask was a persona that the terrified little girl inside of me thought I needed to create in order to feel safe and loved. It protected me for a while, but it soon became my captor. I believed that my world would be secure and that my pain would lessen if I just kept myself small and my surroundings safe. Again, I was wrong and I knew it. I was tired of being wrong . . . and I was tired of being tired.

It was time I did the real work—removing all my masks and healing the little girl inside. It was time to remember who I really was and face my truths. I needed to love myself, listen to myself, and honor my own needs. It took a lot of courage, for very few people understood and supported my choices. No one cared about me—at least that was "my story."

This autobiography was certainly proving true! Reality didn't lie, *right?*

Within two years, I'd lost all my extra weight, my surname, my house, my furniture, my cars, and my money. In return, I found *me.* I had my children and a few prized possessions— namely, some photo albums, my journals, and our clothes. I was still angry at times, but I focused on channeling it, letting it be my driver toward empowerment.

❖ ❖ ❖

It may seem easier to stay hidden because the initial work is tough. But once you step into your power, it becomes easier and easier to create and sustain a life that's based on your terms, dreams, and desires! *What is your mask?*

Who Are You, Really?

The easiest way to identify your trickster, or monster, is by first uncovering the mask(s) you've been wearing. To do so, I want you to ask yourself what you think is the worst thing (or things) to be. What are the most offensive things someone could call you? Don't overanalyze this exercise. Simply be honest with yourself.

What words really trigger you? Fat? Lazy? Stupid? That you're "just like your mother (or father or someone else in your family)"? A slut? A gossip? A slob? Unorganized? Unimportant? A liar? A snob? A fraud? A scammer? An alcoholic or a drug addict? A loser? Maybe self-righteous, messy, cheap, dirty, controlling, or scrawny. Perhaps it's being a home wrecker or a cheater. Useless, jealous, angry, or defensive? Fake? Ugly? Frigid? Weak? A victim? A gold digger? Pathetic? Neurotic? Mean? Bossy? Too shy, too quiet, too emotional, or too boring? An abuser, a lowlife, a loudmouth, or a flake? The list of offensive words is endless.

All you have to do is think about the worst possible things someone could call you. Once you make a list of offensive words, close your eyes and imagine your trickster saying them to you—berating and belittling you. Ask yourself how you've compensated to prove that you aren't these things. How exhausted has it left you? How much energy do you have left over to just be yourself? Are you ready to face yourself and clean up this inner mess?

Once you embrace that your "unacceptable words" are the real fears that you've been carrying around—the corrupted files you've chosen to keep—you can begin to reprogram yourself using more empowered software. Am I saying that you *are* these words? *No!* But I am suggesting that these are the words you'd do anything to avoid being called because deep down they hurt very much. Someone, probably when you were quite young, impressed upon you that these qualities were the worst things to be. *And, yes . . . you have been them at times in your life.*

Be honest—don't you fear that you are or have been any of these words at times? What terrible shame to carry around! What a terrible thing to spend so much of your life—your precious time and energy—trying to cover up and hide! And you are trying to cover them up, *aren't you?*

Just imagine the kind of mask you've created trying to prove that you're not your worst words! Are you now a perfectionist? A people pleaser? A seductress? A tough guy (or gal)? An attention seeker? The list of masks is just as limitless as the list of offensive words. The trouble with wearing a mask, besides the fact that it's so damned exhausting, is that over time, you'll begin to forget who's under the mask. You'll forget who you really are. The mask becomes your "life trap"—the self-destructive pattern, theme, or story that you've adopted since childhood.

Ask yourself the following:

- When did you learn that these "offensive things" were the most unacceptable things to be?

- Whom did you learn this from?

- How did you decide to prove to the world that you aren't these things?

- In what ways did you protect yourself and try to make yourself seem more acceptable, good enough, or worthy?

- What persona or mask have you hidden behind? For example:

  — Are you really shy and insecure but act loud and bold to avoid feeling small?

  — Are you really ashamed and embarrassed but act indifferent and tough to appear strong?

— Do you try to buy people's love, assuming that money and possessions will make you look more important?

— Are you really scared that no one will ever love you, so you act snobbish to avoid being rejected?

— Are you afraid to succeed (and look better than your friends and family), so you sabotage yourself in order to fit in and belong? Do you keep yourself small because no one wants to be around a show-off?

— Are you worried that you're ugly, old, or unattractive, so you exercise like mad, waste hours in front of the mirror, and spend hundreds of dollars on beauty products? Do you wound your spirit even deeper by engaging in meaningless or demeaning sex? (Perhaps it's just to be wanted by someone . . . *anyone*.)

I'm not suggesting that you *really* are these offensive words, but the voice in your head has called you these things so many times that a part of you has actually begun to believe it. And what do you now know about beliefs?

Your beliefs dictate your choices.
Your choices create your life!

You're creating a life based on what you believe from all of the information you've downloaded over the course of your life. Until you *un*install the programs and delete the files that aren't serving you, you can try to reinvent, rewrite, and reprogram your mind; but you'll re-create similar experiences (or patterns) over and over again.

Are All of My Beliefs Bad?

If parts of your life are great, the beliefs surrounding those areas are empowered. If other parts are a struggle, it's an indication that you've adopted false beliefs that are disempowering you. No matter what diet you start, job you land, lover you meet, house you buy, or course you begin, until you discover your true beliefs (and not the politically correct ones you'd like to think you have), you'll keep repeating the same stories of your life! It's predictable.

So let's get down to the nuts and bolts regarding beliefs:

◆ Your thoughts create your beliefs, your beliefs dictate your choices, and your choices create your success (or lack of it).

◆ Since what you believe manifests in reality, you can clearly observe your beliefs just by looking at the results you've gotten.

◆ Your beliefs are telling you what you're worthy of receiving, capable of creating, and skilled at sustaining.

◆ If you believe them, they are true . . . at least they are for you.

◆ You'll always find a way to distort what you perceive to make a belief seem true, even if it's not.

◆ There is no reality—only the reality you believe.

◆ Choose to see things differently, and they will be.

The good news is that it's not your fault that your life—or parts of it—keeps being sabotaged. The bad news is that it's *you* who's doing the destruction. You're the computer programmer, and only you can choose to fix the operating system.

Does this make sense?

Somewhere along the way, you heard, saw, and decided that you were worthy of receiving some things, capable of achieving others, and not so good at sustaining most of it. You decided what you should look like, act like, and be like; how much money you should make; how a lover should treat you; what the world should do for you; and what is expected from you in return. Your experiences continue to reaffirm this to you, making it even more believable. And today, you are a culmination of your life's experiences—your downloadable files.

You are the sum of your beliefs: your parents' beliefs, your siblings', grandparents', teachers', friends', and so on. Not to mention you've watched plenty of television, read magazines, and have been told exactly what you should want, be, and do. *Thank you everyone! You've told me what to believe, and I've believed it!*

It's time to clean out the old beliefs and rewrite your story, letting go of the idea of what you wished you were or wished they were, of what he should have done, or what she promised to do. They didn't, you aren't, they aren't, it isn't—*oh, well . . . let's get on with it!*

It is what it is! Don't beat yourself up. Just clean it up and begin reinventing!

❖ ❖ ❖   REINVENT YOUR STYLE   ❖ ❖ ❖

Who better to ask how to reinvent style than my dear friend Korby Banner, celebrity photographer and international makeup artist, whose portfolio includes Brad Pitt, Johnny Depp, Harrison Ford, Sophia Loren, Lenny Kravitz, Jennifer Lopez, Tony Bennett, Joan Collins, Angelina Jolie, Viggo Mortensen, Jessica Alba, Heath Ledger, Beyoncé, and Justin Timberlake? His work is seen daily in more than 25 countries in five languages on *Style by Jury,* a hit TV makeover show that helps women find a new life through self-transformation.

I asked Korby how a makeover can be a great catalyst to help us change other aspects of our lives. He told me this: "The fringe benefit of reinventing yourself physically is that it changes the world around you. Your new image radiates confidence; it attracts better work offers and social invitations, and generally wins new friends. The odd revelation is that many of those people would probably have been your friend before, but you didn't feel deserving or worthy."

He went on to say: "If a woman desires to reinvent herself, it all starts in the mirror! Everyone strives to have high self-esteem (not an easy task in a critical and competitive world that plainly illustrates a person's shortcomings). The thing to remember is that you should only compare yourself to *you*. Being the best you can be is admirable and achievable. All individuals possess qualities that make him or her unique and wonderful. Competing against airbrushed models on magazine covers is futile, and obsessing over skinny Hollywood actresses is silly. Know for sure that being healthy and strong is better than being half-starved and neurotic!"

Well said, Korby!

He went on to give me a few of his top beauty tips:

◆   Proper grooming is essential.

◆   Well-cared-for skin has a luminescence and
     glowing radiance.

- Using sun protection when you're young is vital for mature beauty.

- Keep your smile white—it enhances an overall youthful appearance.

- When your longer hair starts looking frizzy or stringy, go for a shorter sexy style that showcases your features.

- Update your makeup every five years. As you age, less product and lighter colors are usually more becoming—darker definition on an older face can appear harsh.

- Well-arched brows are advantageous to a mature face.

- Eyeliner on top eyelids is great for all ages, whereas full liner on bottom lids is normally best suited for the younger eye.

- Matte (versus frosted) shadow will de-emphasize fine texture lines on mature eyelids.

- Keep your lips and surrounding skin well moisturized.

- To stay fresh looking, always drink in moderation and don't smoke. Harsh but true!

- Eat a good breakfast every day!

- Take that dance class you've always wanted to.

And Korby stresses that more important than all of the exterior dressings are the three vital traits to being perceived as beautiful your whole life:

1. Good posture
2. Kind eyes
3. A genuine smile

What Are You So Afraid Of?

You don't need to fear your trickster (or what some refer to as the ego) because it's not your enemy, just as the monster wasn't an enemy, initially, to Dr. Frankenstein. The monster saw the doctor as his father—his creator—but when his father turned his back on him, he became angry and afraid.

Viewing your ego as something you must annihilate will only create more fear and resistance within you. Your ego will fight for its life, even if it means destroying you, its creator! It doesn't mean to hurt or berate you. It was formed when you were young—when you didn't know that you were connected to a Divine Universal Collective Energy, or what some call God.

Besides, your ego has served a vital purpose in your life. Imagine being in a dark alley late at night as three thugs approach you. It's probably your ego, or your trickster, that will save your butt, simply because it's the most primitive part of you. But since most of your life isn't spent in a dark alley, you don't need (or want) to constantly be in survival mode!

(*Note:* If you do live in a "scary world of survival," it's time to leave it for a more empowered way of living, and only you can do this for yourself. *You must!*)

❖ ❖ ❖

When I first uncovered my greatest fears and the ways I tried to suppress them, it was incredible. It was almost as if a light had been turned on and I could see clearly! I imagined what my trickster looked like and, surprisingly, the image of a mean, old, self-righteous nun came to my mind. My nun truly believed that if I played it small and acted "proper," I'd look good, people would like me, and I'd be "enough." Sometimes she won and I'd act like a lovely little martyr. At other times in my life, I completely rebelled and reacted in ways similar to my trigger words. I became my worst fears and would shame myself more! (*Or maybe it was my ego that would shame me more?*)

At first I yelled at my nun and told her to go away and leave me alone, but then I realized that as long I saw her as my opponent, I'd always be at odds with myself. Since this mean old lady was inside of me, and a part of me, as long as I resisted her, she would persist.

So I decided to view her through new lenses—the eyes of my spirit. What a different image I saw! She was merely a frightened old woman who was terrified that I wouldn't be getting into heaven. She really believed that money was evil, sex was only for procreation, and having too much fun was the path paved to hell. Girls shouldn't have daring haircuts or wear makeup and short skirts! The nun was taught to care most about what everyone else thought. She was a martyr, but she didn't know any better and was only afraid. I realized she simply needed love and reassurance.

Once I embraced the idea that my nun wasn't my enemy (*I'd created her; she didn't create me*) and that fighting her would only give her more power with the resistance I was creating within myself, I was able to understand the secret to *all* of creation:

Life can only develop in perfect equilibrium depending upon the need of the individual, thus explaining the necessity for contrast or duality. It's the sole way we can discover our own tipping point— the only way to expand and grow.

I'd spent so much of my life believing that everything "bad" needed to be avoided—not realizing that without darkness there's no light, without light there's no darkness. There's a reason for everything, even when we don't understand it. It's our self-righteousness that fools us into believing otherwise. We're afraid of the tipping point! We run from the edge, afraid to fall.

I'd created my nun—my ego—because, initially, I needed protection . . . and she did protect me! She taught me how to cover up my guilt and shame. She showed me how to be strong, disciplined, focused, and driven. She helped me make "proper" and "good" choices and steered me in the right direction. She kept me safe from the edge—safe from falling . . . *or flying.*

Now when my nun starts yelling at me—belittling, judging, or trying to condemn me for anything, whether it's sipping a glass of wine, telling someone no, or making passionate love— I take her by the hand and sit her down in a rocking chair, place a blanket around her shoulders, and get her a cup of tea. "Everything will be okay," I lovingly tell her. "I'm just being me, and being me is perfectly okay."

❖ ❖ ❖

What if you decided to make peace with yourself—to make peace with your fears, with your worst words? What if you decided to "live and let live"? What if you were determined to really live? Explore? Fall? Fly? Become the authentic *you*— without protective gear?

Think of how much energy, peace, excitement, bliss, and freedom you'd experience. Imagine what your life could be— what could blossom! You'd have the personal space to do the things you *really* want to do . . . not what you think you need to do in order to keep up with the image you've created. *Doesn't this sound wonderful?*

Stop Resisting

We already know that we can't reprogram new beliefs unless we truly believe that they're safe and beneficial. To "outsmart" the ego (*not destroy it*), we simply need to uncover why it believes the things that it does—in other words, we have to examine all of its perceived benefits, then create new motivators that it will recognize as even *more* beneficial.

Do you understand how important it is that you don't resist your ego?

Once you comprehend that certain instructions from your ego have helped you, you can thank your ego and explain that you're going to try a different, more enlightened and empowered way of doing things. It will resist change, so be prepared. Your ego is just afraid—like Dr. Frankenstein's monster. You may sense that it's fighting for its life, but simply put a blanket around its shoulders, too. Embrace it and know that it too *is alive!*

Trick the Trickster!

You've probably realized what you've lost out on in your life by believing some of the things you have, but can you see what you've gained? If you can do this—understand your payoff—then you can outsmart your own mind and tame your beast!

I'm sure you can see why you created your ego in the first place. Like many well-intentioned ideas gone bad (just like Dr. Frankenstein's), you now have to learn how to outsmart the trickster by understanding, accepting, and even loving it. Here's an example of me coaching one of my clients through this process:

> *Crystal:* What have you lost out on in your life because of your old beliefs?
>
> *Karen:* Everything!
>
> *Crystal:* Like what? Give me some examples.
>
> *Karen:* Well, I never get to see what I can truly achieve because I'm too afraid to try, too afraid to make a mistake or do anything wrong.
>
> *Crystal:* Good for you for recognizing that! Now, what have you gained by holding on to your old beliefs?
>
> *Karen:* Nothing! Absolutely nothing—I'm miserable.
>
> *Crystal:* Well, that can't be entirely true because you wouldn't have held on to them for this long unless you were getting some kind of payoff. Really think about it. Examine some of your self-limiting

beliefs: Where have they helped you out at times? How have they benefited you?

Karen (laughing): Well, I guess I've gotten attention.

Crystal: What else? How else have they helped you? Protected you?

Karen: I've been able to play it safe and never step out of my comfort zone. Everyone around me thinks I'm smart and logical . . . that I've got it together, because I never do anything wrong or risky.

Crystal: How's that working for you?

Karen: Well, in one way, I guess, it's okay. I mean . . . I don't really ever fail because I never do something if I think I might not be successful. But it's also not so good at times—I mean, for my life . . . for my dreams . . . for my marriage . . . my children. *(She begins to softly cry.)*

Crystal: Why, Karen? Why is it not so good for your kids and your marriage?

Karen (really crying now): Because, well, if something doesn't work out . . . I can blame other people because they weren't there to help me. Things are never *my* fault. At least I never admit I'm wrong. I can always find a way to blame someone else. And I do blame everyone else—even my kids. *(She pauses.)* I mean . . . how can I blame my kids? They're just kids . . . innocent children. And my husband loves me. I know he does, and I'm so hard on him. . . .

Does this sound familiar?

When it doesn't have to be our fault, we can blame it on anyone other than ourselves. If we can, at least, be *un*account-able, that means others are accountable. Our problems aren't our own: "It's not my fault. I didn't create this mess. It's my husband's fault. He's such a control freak!"

Is it also possible that if it's not your fault, you don't have to do the work and you don't have to change? You can blame. You can be the victim. You can get attention for all the terrible things that have happened to you. You can point the finger because you're an innocent bystander in your own life. *Poor you!* The trouble with this, though, is that if you don't make the decisions for your life, how can you fix anything? If you aren't responsible for your own life, who is?

Here's the honest truth: *No one is coming to save you.* But guess what? You never needed saving. You just needed the right software in order to make peace with yourself—with your ego—and then you can save yourself! Before you can do so, you need to realize who your voice is.

Close your eyes and picture what your ego looks like. Get a very good visual of the kinds of things it says to you and how it would look if it were an actual person. What do you see? Can you describe your ego? Is it young, old, mean, or weak?

The next time you start feeling or hearing yourself repeating its lies, remind yourself that it doesn't know the real you; it doesn't know that your spirit is strong, capable, willing, accepting, loving, and completely empowered. Your spirit will never trick you. (I'll explain who your spirit is and how to hear its voice in the coming chapters.)

Begin by dialoguing with your ego, explaining to it that you're both going to be okay, so it should stop worrying so much! It just needs your reassurance and love.

21 Days to a New You

The next step to reinvent, rewrite, and reprogram your mind—in order for you to rebuild whatever parts of your life aren't working—isn't as hard as you think, but you do need to know what it is that you want to install.

Most people know what they *don't want* and unknowingly focus most of their energy on it: "I don't want to be fat! I don't want to be broke all the time! I don't want to fight with him anymore! I don't like my job! I don't like the way my parents talk to me! I don't want to be a victim!" To reprogram your mind, you have to focus on what you *do* want! Since you already know what you don't like—the things that aren't working in your life—imagine the complete opposite. By doing so, you can figure out what you really desire. This takes a willing spirit to surrender the need to be right—a spirit that will allow you to let go of your story. You must be willing to question almost everything you once believed and examine anything that has held you back, hurt you, stopped you, demeaned you, or controlled you to see if it's real or learned. Then ask yourself: *How can I be so certain it's true?*

What you'll realize, if you do the work, is that all of your "reasons" for failing—your excuses, fears, frustrations, and limitations—are simply beliefs that can be changed. All you have to ask yourself is if there's anyone else who has gone through something similar to you but has overcome it. Can you view it through those lenses and see the empowered outcome? If so, then you know you can do it differently, if you choose to.

If what you're doing isn't getting you what you want, change your mind. Stop repeating your story. Stop telling it to anyone who will listen. Stop using it to justify why you are the way you are or why things are the way they are. Give it up!

An easy way to achieve this is to make a list of all the beliefs that are holding you back—take stock of everything that isn't working in your life. Without any judgment, use the Circle-of-Life Assessment from Chapter 1 as your guide, and let your results show you the truth about what you believe, positive and negative!

Let me give you some examples:

My old life mirrored to me someone who believed that:

1. *I don't trust men. (Proof: I attract unfaithful mates!)*

2. *I'm fat. (Proof: I keep gaining weight and can't lose it!)*

3. *I'm not good with money. (Proof: My bank account is always overdrawn!)*

4. *I'll never get along with my parents. (Proof: I haven't talked to them in two years!)*

5. *My siblings and I don't see eye to eye. (Proof: We argue at every gathering!)*

6. *I hate exercising. (Proof: I rarely work out, and when I do I resent it!)*

7. *I don't like drinking water. (Proof: I rarely drink water. I hate the taste!)*

8. *I don't believe that I can lose weight and keep it off. (Proof: It's a constant battle that I've never won!)*

9. *I don't think that thin, sexy women are good mothers. (Proof: My mother was sexy, and she was trouble!)*

10. *Money is hard to make. (Proof: I'm very smart, yet I can't seem to make enough to pay my bills!)*

Next to each self-limiting belief, write down what it has cost you, as well as how it has served you or helped you. (You need to understand the gifts that some of your beliefs have given you to understand why you've held on to them.)

Then make a new list of beliefs by creating a new story for your life. Start by writing down the opposite of all your old self-limiting beliefs. For example:

My new story is:

1. *I trust men and I'm excited about being in a committed, loving, healthy relationship.*

2. *I'm fit, strong, sexy, and empowered!*

3. *I'm great with money!*

4. *I get along with my parents and forgive them for any mistakes they made. They're human! Everyone makes mistakes.*

5. *My siblings and I agree to disagree sometimes, but we love each other anyway!*

6. *I enjoy exercising because I know what it does for me!*

7. *I drink plenty of water because it makes me feel incredible!*

8. *I've lost weight, and I'll keep it off!*

9. *I'm thin and sexy, and I'm still a great mother and wife!*

10. *I know that earning money is simply an exchange of energy. I easily make plenty of it!*

Beside each positive statement, write down the ways in which they'll benefit your life. Visualize yourself living this new way. *How do you feel?*

Read your list out loud at least twice a day for 21 days. It takes this much time to reprogram the synaptic pathways in your brain—that is, 21 days to create a habit. Think of it this way: *21 days to a new you!*

Affirmations work but only after you've cleaned out the negative messages that have been directing your life. Remember that it doesn't matter what was . . . what matters is what will be.

This is your opportunity to become anything you choose to be!

Chapter Three

EXECUTE YOUR PLAN

> *"Whatever you can do or dream you can, begin it.*
> *Boldness has genius, power,*
> *and magic in it."*
>
> — *Johann Wolfgang von Goethe*

At my SWAT (Simply Woman Accredited Training) Institute, we teach our coaches how to create a comprehensive "Prescription for Success." It's not possible to teach you everything in one book, but I do want to help you create your own "R_x for Success" that will be life transforming.

As your family, friends, career, and other interests grow and change, your success plan will keep you on track, ensuring that everything is balanced. When life gets too chaotic, it will serve as your map, showing you how to get back on the right path.

Your R_x for Success will be made up of seven different components:

1. Your Current Lifestyle Assessment
2. Your Values
3. Your Dreams and Desires
4. Your Drivers
5. Your Priorities
6. Your Weaknesses
7. Your Commitments

Your R$_x$ for Success

To create your Prescription for Success, you need to get a three-ring binder with paper, seven dividers, colored markers and pencils, a pen, glue, scissors, photos of yourself and those you love, and some old magazines. Start by creating your R$_x$ for Success title page. Be creative! Then label the seven dividers and put it all into your binder, with blank sheets of paper between each section.

Let's go through each of the prescriptions:

1. Your Current Lifestyle Assessment

You can't create an effective plan without knowing what's been working in your life and what hasn't. In Chapter 1, you took an honest look at your current situation. You examined your Circle of Life and realized where you still need to do some cleaning and healing in order to create more balance. If you haven't done this assessment yet, go back and do it, and then transfer the results into your workbook.

This is also the place where you can insert your old beliefs from Chapter 2 and record the details of specific areas that you'd like to change. For example, take a picture of yourself in a bathing suit and record your measurements and weight, your blood pressure, resting heart rate, and cholesterol ratio. List your assets and liabilities, plus your bank-account balance. Take a picture of the rooms in your home that are in need of a purge: your garage, basement, closets, and so on. You can also record any other areas of your life that concern you, such as the number of cigarettes you smoke per day, fast-food stops you make per week, or alcoholic drinks you consume. Date it.

You need to have a very clear picture of where you currently are for three main reasons:

1. It shows you the truth. You can keep convincing yourself that your situation isn't so bleak, but a picture says a thousand words (and bank statements don't lie). It is what it is!

2. It helps you track your progress. As your life changes, you'll continue to record your progress, documenting what's working and what isn't. Plus, this is important to have in case you need to

uncover any flaws in your plan (this is explained in Part II).

3. It offers you proof! A few months from now, you'll forget exactly where you were. You may cringe today, but one day, not so far off, these numbers and pictures will be evidence of your extraordinary transformation.

2. Your Values

Once you know and understand your personal values, you can consult them whenever you need to make a key decision, such as:

◆ Should you accept the new job you've been offered? Does it align with your values?

◆ Do the people closest to you know the *real you,* and do their values align with yours?

◆ Are you being selfish or self-loving when you say no to certain things?

Your list of values provides a shortcut for making decisions spontaneously and intuitively. In the beginning, when you're confronted with a choice, you can pull out your list and ask yourself, *What would a person with these values do in this situation?* Over time, it will become second nature to know when to say yes or no.

A simple but powerful way to figure out your values is to read over the following list of words (see next page), and pick out any that excite or intrigue you. Hold no judgment about whether they measure up to what society, your parents, mate, family, and children (and so on) have told you are the "right" values to have. The secret to being empowered comes not from living on the right path, but from following the path that's right for you!

I review the list every few months and circle the words that jump out at me. I tend to focus on the same words, but occasionally, a new one will really light me up. Now it's your turn: Look at the following list, and say each word out loud. Ask yourself: *Do I love something about this word?* If so, jot it down immediately—no questions asked, no explanation needed!

Values

Abundance, acceptance, accomplishment, achievement, acknowledgment, adoration, adventure, affection, affluence, ambition, appreciation, approachability, assertiveness, attractiveness, awareness, awe, balance, beauty, belonging, bliss, boldness, bravery, brilliance, calmness, celebrity, charm, cheerfulness, clarity, cleanliness, clearheadedness, cleverness, closeness, comfort, commitment, compassion, confidence, connection, consciousness, consistency, contentment, contribution, conviction, coolness, courage, creativity, curiosity, daring, dependability, desire, determination, devotion, devoutness, dignity, directness, discipline, discovery, discretion, diversity, dreaming, dynamic, eagerness, ecstasy, education, effectiveness, efficiency, elation, elegance, eloquence, empathy, encouragement, endurance, energy, enjoyment, entertainment, enthusiasm, excellence, excitement, exhilaration, experience, expertise, exploration, expressiveness, extravagance, faith, fame, family, fashion, fearlessness, ferocity, fidelity, fierceness, feistiness, financial independence, firmness, fitness, flexibility, flow, fluency, focus, fortitude, frankness, freedom, friendliness, fun, generosity, gentility, giving, grace, gratitude, gregariousness, growth, guidance, happiness, harmony, health, heart, help, heroism, holiness, honesty, honor, hopefulness, humility, humor, imagination, independence, ingenuity, inquisitiveness, insightfulness, inspiration, integrity, intelligence, intensity, intimacy, intuition, intuitiveness, inventiveness, joy, justice, keenness, kindness, knowledge, leadership, learning, legacy, liberation, liberty, liveliness, logic, longevity, love, loyalty, majesty, making a difference, mastery, maturity, mindfulness, modesty, motivation, mysteriousness, neatness, nerve, open-mindedness, openness, optimism, order, organization, originality, outlandishness, outrageousness, passion, peace, perceptiveness, perfection, perkiness, perseverance, persistence, persuasiveness, philanthropy, piety, playfulness, pleasantness, pleasure, poise, polish, popularity, potency, power, practicality, precision, preparedness, presence, privacy, proactive, professionalism, prosperity, prudence, punctuality, purity, realism, reason, reasonableness, recognition, recreation, refinement, reflection, relaxation, reliability, religiousness, resilience, resolution, resolve, resourcefulness, respect, rest, restraint, reverence, riches, rigor, sacredness, sacrifice, sagacity, saintliness, satisfaction, security, self-control, selflessness, self-reliance, sensitivity, sensuality, serenity, service, sex, sexuality, sharing, shrewdness, significance, silence, silliness, simplicity, sincerity, skillfulness, solidarity, solitude, soundness, speed, spirit, spirituality, spontaneity, spunk, stability, stillness, strength, success, support, synergy, temperance, thankfulness, thoroughness, thoughtfulness, timeliness, tranquility, transcendence, trust, trustworthiness, truth, understanding, uniqueness, unity, usefulness, valor, victory, vigor, virtue, vision, vitality, vivacity, warmth, watchfulness, wealth, wildness, willingness, winning, wisdom, wittiness, wonder, youthfulness, zeal

Great job! Now look over your words, and narrow them down to your top ten. This can be hard, especially if you love many of them. Using a scale from 1 to 10 (10 being the best), and without thinking too much about it, say the word out loud and give it a number. You'll quickly narrow it down to the ones that you resonate with the most. Now you have your top-10 words!

They are perfect . . . *for you!* Don't try to understand why they're perfect or what you need to do with them at this point. Don't worry about how they're going to manifest in your life. Just know that these are the words that lift your spirit—the things you need *right now* to create *your* perfect balance so that you feel aligned, grounded, and empowered. They represent your "end" values.

End values are different from *means values.* We've all heard people say things like: "My job is just a means to an end." Most of us focus too much on our "means," actually believing that these things "mean" something important about us. What really matters in the end is what lights us up and inspires us. When we're inspired, we're "in spirit."

It's not the car, house, money, status job, or lover (all means values) that will make you feel empowered. It's the safety, security, freedom, achievement, and/or passion that fills you with happiness and satisfaction. The good feelings, not good things, are what your spirit longs for.

If you really believe that other people or things will make you feel successful, you're still being an innocent bystander in your own life. With that mentality, you can easily have your success and happiness swept right out from under your feet: The car can break down, the house could be destroyed in a fire, the stock market can crash, or your lover may leave you. Rotten things can affect your outer world, but they don't have to ruin your inner world. Losing "stuff" can actually set you free, which is a major cleansing! (Sometimes the Universe will step in when it realizes that we don't have the courage to make a necessary change and do it for us!)

Please let me clearly state this: I'm not suggesting that money doesn't make things easier or that a beautiful, committed lover isn't one of the best things in life, but we must know who we truly are and what we truly need in order to feel empowered and make choices that will bring us genuine contentment. When we know and trust in ourselves and make choices that always maintain our own perfect balance (which can be challenging even at the best of times), we'll never again be at the mercy of anything or anyone.

The key is realizing what's necessary for you to stay balanced. Your needs will be different from mine—or from anyone else's, for that matter. What's easy for you may be overwhelming for me, or vice versa. The secret is learning to listen to yourself.

The dictionary defines the word *authenticity* as being "true to one's own spirit or personality." *Hmm . . . being true to our own spirit, yet what do most of us do?* We focus on our means (the job, money, house, car, lover) and neglect our soul's priorities. We're afraid to trust that everything will work out if we honor ourselves and acknowledge our deepest needs, desires, and wants. Most of us are people pleasers at a huge cost to ourselves. We feel selfish or controlling if we say no to something that doesn't align with our values . . . yet this is what integrity means. This is what an authentic person does! You say what you mean and mean what you say.

If you neglect your end values, you aren't living in integrity. You're not being authentic . . . and you probably feel it! Nevertheless, so many keep faking it by not honoring themselves—by playing it small and safe—and then wonder why they never feel empowered! The late great mythologist Joseph Campbell wrote: "Follow your bliss and doors will open where there were no doors before."

When you give your spirit what it truly desires, doors open. (Not always the minute you want them to, but regardless, you always feel authentic and empowered.) You'll always be the creator of your destiny. And that's not to say your needs and desires won't change! When God created the Universe, everything was designed to maintain a perfect homeostasis, or balance. Chaos is when things become extremely unbalanced. Humans have since created many imbalances in this world. Throughout your life, as you continue to create your personal universe, you must continually check in (every few months) to maintain your own harmony. When things become unbalanced, you'll feel a sense of inner chaos. This is a gift! Don't wait until life shuts you down to restore your truth.

In Section 2 of your R_x for Success, write down your top-10 words and how each one makes you feel. Be sure to date it. Flip through magazines and cut out pictures or words that resonate with your feelings. Notice how much fun this step is! Be sure to check back every few months to see if your words have changed.

Be What It Is You Want!

Look at your top-10 words and imagine yourself as a person who exemplifies all of them. How would this individual act, dress, and speak? How would her hair look? How would she carry herself? What kind of career would she have? How would the people in her life treat her? What kind of partner or lover would she have? What would her daily life be like?

Get a visual of her. Can you see her? Do you feel her?

This is your spirit. She's inside of you! You simply need to acknowledge her and align your choices with the ones she'd make, and *you'll be this person again.*

Find photos in magazines or on the Internet that exemplify this person, or if you're feeling creative, draw a picture of her. Get your hair cut like her, buy clothes she'd wear, act the way she'd act, speak the way she'd speak, and so on. Choose to be her now! Sometimes I remind my clients that they need to "fake it till they make it." Soon you'll actually believe yourself and feel authentic being *you!*

3. Your Dreams and Desires

In the must-have book *Think and Grow Rich,* Napoleon Hill wrote that "the starting point of all achievement is *desire*"— specifically, a burning desire.

What is it that you want to be successful at? How badly do you want to succeed? How badly do you want to sustain that success? Why should the world pay you for your ideas and dreams? What's your value, and what do you feel is a fair exchange for your worth?

Making money, just like loving someone, is merely an exchange of values or energy. Your product, (*or you*), resonates at a certain frequency to be exchanged with a currency of relative energy. For every action, there is an equal and opposite reaction! This applies to creating and sustaining money, love, friends, opportunity, and so on. This law applies to all people, not just certain individuals. It doesn't differentiate among nationality, sex, age, or income. True desire is akin to passion. When you're truly passionate about something, it becomes effortless to think about it, dream about it, crave it, visualize it, want it, see it, breathe it . . . and then create it. Sir Isaac Newton was once asked how he discovered the law of gravitation, and he replied: "By thinking about it all the time." Whatever you give your attention to, you also give power to. Where attention goes, energy flows . . . and *it* grows—good or bad!

Creation is the alignment of your desire in thought, word, and action. It was born out of the contrast you've been living. To sustain what you've created takes a lot more than having desire, however. It requires all the steps in Part I, along with unwavering focus, perseverance, and a willingness to continue to rework your plan, if need be.

The trouble with most people is that they don't truly love what they're creating. Their work is a chore—a means to an end—and they have no dream, no vision. Persevering is painful. Oftentimes, too many other things get in the way. They love the idea of having money, for example, but they don't love what they're doing to create that money. No different are those who dream of getting married and having children, but settle for a partner they don't passionately desire. It's the "means" they're after, and when the marriage fails, they wonder what went wrong.

Moreover, if you don't love what you're doing (or who you're doing it with) you'll have a very difficult time sustaining what you've created. You'll always be tempted by other opportunities or people, and keeping your focus will be extremely challenging.

When you provide a product or service that was created with deep passion, however, its potential return is high. *It is . . . truth—you can't deny it.* When you love someone with all of your heart and soul, your potential return is also high.

Conversely, if you create a product or service or engage in a relationship that lacks integrity, the potential return is low. You get what you give! There's no such reality as "something for nothing." If you don't like what you've been getting, it's time to do the work: cleaning up your messes, rewriting your future, and developing your own net worth. The great American writer, poet, naturalist, and early transcendentalist Henry David Thoreau explained it in this way: "The cost of a thing is the amount of what I will call life which is required to be exchanged for it, immediately or in the long run."

Dream Your Greatest Dream

Now that you know what your true values are—what you love, what your spirit needs, and what lights you up—I want you to dream your greatest dream. The catch is that you *must not settle for anything less of yourself!* This is one of the most powerful secrets of true empowerment. Know what you want, know who you are, and never sell out on yourself!

One of the best ways I've found to stay true to myself and my dreams is by thinking from the end—that is, thinking about how I want to be remembered. My ex-husband used to tell me that I had a death fantasy. I didn't. What I had (and still possess) was a deep desire to leave a legacy . . . an important legacy. This is one of my end values.

My deep desire enabled me to fast forward to the end of my life and look back. It compelled me to think about the things that mattered most to me, and that takes courage. Not all my friends, family, or partners could understand my values or priorities. They often thought I was too driven, too serious, too focused, too ambitious, too . . . *something!* But for me, following my passion was natural; my dreaming drove me, and settling for less wasn't an option. I felt guilty at times for choosing my dreams over my lover's wants, but it was my truth. Thankfully, I now have a husband who understands me, loves me, and would never make me choose between him and my passions.

The questions that often came up for me were things such as:

◆ How will my life have mattered?

◆ How will I have impacted others in a positive and significant way?

◆ Will I have done a great job raising my children, inspiring them to live magnificent and purpose-driven lives? Will they know how loved and special they were?

◆ Will my husband know how much I loved and appreciated him?

◆ As I stand before my Maker, how will I feel?

◆ How will my friends and family remember me?

◆ Will I have any regrets at the end of my life? If so, how can I clean them up now?

I encourage you to think from the end as well. Ask yourself these or similar questions and see what comes up for you. Remember: *If you can dream it, you can achieve it!*

I also encourage you to think about the "means" values that you've often dreamed of having. There's nothing wrong with wanting a beautiful car or a house on the ocean; it becomes a problem only when you value those things more than you value your relationships—more than you value people.

Put your answers in Section 3. Then create a collage or a vision map with pictures of yourself (one as a child is ideal!) and the people you love, and cut out images from magazines that remind you of your dreams and values ("end" and "means"). Date it. It will be so much fun when you look back—even just a year from now—to see how many of your desires are already materializing!

But remember, as you look at what it is that you want most, ask yourself if your personal output equals your hoped-for potential input. In other words, are you giving *enough?* You must determine what you intend to give in return for the things— possessions and feelings—you dream about possessing.

4. Your Drivers

Empowered people often have quite admirable "drivers"— the motivators, or reasons that compel them to do or achieve something. Disempowered people may want to have noble drivers, but they usually don't and understandably can't . . . they're disempowered! Paying the rent or keeping the electricity running might be what motivates them to get up and go to work each day, rather than building shelters or helping to alleviate world hunger.

When I have a client who's resonating in a place of shame, for example, and she tells me that her driver is "self-care," I tell her that, in my opinion, she'll fail. Sustaining self-care requires an enormous amount of self-love—something that she doesn't have much of yet.

The best way to understand this journey of empowerment is to compare it to traveling across the country. If you were in New York and wanted to get to California, whether you fly, drive, bike, or walk, you'd have to pass through many states. In this journey, the states are "states of emotion." If shame was New York and California was love, just imagine how many various states you'd experience along the way. And just like driving a vehicle across the country, on this empowerment journey, you'd also need enough fuel to get there. Your "driver" is your fuel. It's what propels you through each state.

Sometimes we stay in one place longer than we'd like to, but for whatever reason, we need to be there. Eventually, we gather enough fuel to move on, or sadly, we stay stuck in a state we really didn't want to live in. Our drivers will always match our level of consciousness—or level of empowerment—and that's perfectly okay. *It is what it is.*

According to Dr. David Hawkins's brilliant book *Power vs. Force,* the states of emotion are levels of consciousness; they are both measurable and progressive. The progression isn't an arithmetic equation but a logarithmic measurement, meaning that an increase of even a few points represents a major advance in power. The lowest resonating state is shame with a calibration of 20. It progresses into guilt with a measurement of 30, then to apathy at 50, grieving is 75, fear 100, desire 125, anger 150, and pride 175.

Pride is the *highest* level of the *lower* levels of consciousness. A person who resonates in pride is more empowered than someone who's afraid and guilt driven. As Hawkins points out: "Pride can pull someone from the gutter or spur a nation on to war," but resonating in pride is certainly *not* empowered nor is it where you'd want to remain. *Imagine always needing to have all of the answers to prove you're better than everyone else!* The higher levels of consciousness begin with courage, which calibrates at 200, and moves up into willingness at 310, and acceptance 350, with our destination of love at a whopping 500.

The important thing to keep in mind is that although we'd all love to just teleport ourselves to the "City of Love" the way they would in *Star Trek,* we can't. Compare moving through your emotional states (or the levels of consciousness) to turning up a dimmer switch on the dining-room wall: you know you can't get to a level five without first passing one, two, three, and four. If you're resonating at a 20 in consciousness—shame—you must move through your feelings of guilt, apathy, grief, fear, desire, anger, pride, and into courage before you can ever get close to level 500 . . . love. *Does this make sense?*

What Is Your Driver?

When I was a teenager, my driver was to escape my terrible shame and guilt. Shame says, "Who I am is no good." Guilt says, "What I did is no good." I became a people pleaser. It drove me and kept me very busy being busy, constantly trying to look perfect, act perfect, and be perfect. It mattered so much that others liked and accepted me, even though I often felt that if they knew the real me, they wouldn't love me so much. But I thought that if I did enough, I'd be enough.

By my mid-20s, I found myself completely exhausted. I'd become a martyr: *Poor me! Look at all that I do for everyone! Isn't someone going to notice how wonderful I am and take care of me?* After the birth of my children, I remember feeling so vulnerable. I'd given up my career and was dependent on my husband. There was no balance. I'd become a victim! Blaming others—especially my parents—felt better than beating up on myself (something I'd done for long enough), but it also kept me stuck and stagnant. Staying in the "City of Apathy" robbed me of my dignity, as I waited for others to recognize the worth that I couldn't yet see in myself. I didn't want to go back to people pleasing, but in order to move past this state, I knew that I'd have to gather up more fuel and face myself. I'd need to face my demons and clean up the mess I'd tried to forget. For a while, it was easier to "eat away" my pain; and ice cream, chocolate bars, and soda became my new best friends. They loved me when no one else did.

And then late one night, while nursing my youngest daughter, something inside of me seemed to crack. The dam broke and the crying began, as all of the bottled-up sorrow poured out of me. I sobbed for what I'd wished my life "would have been," "should have been," and "ought to have been." I sobbed for the mistakes I'd made—the ways I'd let myself and others down. My breakdown was my breakthrough. I'd held in so much pain for so many years, and the release was overwhelming.

Finally, when the tears began to dry, I realized it was time to clean up my body, my house, my mind, and my finances, as well as face my fears. Living this way wasn't living at all. My daughters deserved more. I deserved more.

The funny thing about desire is that once you know, *you know!* And when you don't get what you *know you want* and *know you deserve,* frustration sets in.

I quickly realized that wanting wasn't enough. Wanting wasn't going to get me to a better place. Wanting, without taking action, only made me more frustrated! I was sick and tired of my old excuses and justifications. I was fed up with my story, with myself! I was done with blaming, waiting, and crying. My desire had shifted into anger—not anger as in the yelling, hitting, screaming kind. It was more like the anger portrayed in movies such as *Rocky, Remember the Titans, Chariots of Fire,* or my newest favorite, *Slumdog Millionaire.* Channeled anger has a way of creating massive momentum!

Oh . . . I was pissed! I'd entered the "City of Anger," and no one liked it, especially my poor husband! He wanted the old version of me back: the people pleaser, lovely hostess, good cook, housekeeper, and subservient sex goddess. *Couldn't I just get dinner ready and talk about all this stuff another time?*

I became indignant, knowing that the old version of myself was never coming back. I'd never allow anyone to abuse, neglect, or mistreat me again! *Who was this woman staring back at me now?* She both scared and excited me. In no time, I lost the 80 pounds I gained with my pregnancies, I began writing every day in my journal, and I started to stand up for myself, while thinking from the end perspective. My husband needed to change, too, if I was to stay. He didn't. I did.

It took a lot of courage, but I eventually left my husband, took my two young daughters with me, and set out to self-publish my first book. (My husband never allowed me to invest any of our money into my dreams or goals; instead, he'd squander it on "get rich quick" schemes—most of them illegal. I realized that I'd never be able to do the work I wanted to do with women and families with *my* marriage so out of integrity.) Some of my family members tried to shame me *(how could there have been problems since I hadn't told anyone about them?!),* and my husband tried to blame me, but I knew I had a destiny and this *wasn't* it! I had faith that where there's a will there's a way. My will drove me. I believed that I had a purpose, and I finally started to believe in myself.

I began to recite "The Serenity Prayer" each day:

Grant me the serenity to accept the things I cannot change,
the courage to change the things I can,
and the wisdom to know the difference.

Something very powerful was happening: It didn't matter anymore if others liked me, although it seemed that I was getting more respect and admiration than ever before. I liked who I was becoming! I knew I was special. I knew that I was a magnificent child of God, and playing it small wasn't going to cut it any longer. I also acknowledged that my parents were special—actually, incredibly dynamic—people. They never set out to intentionally hurt me or my siblings. They were very young when they got married and started raising a family, and the problems in their relationship soon became overwhelming.

My husband wasn't a *totally* bad guy either. He had been abused growing up and came from a very poor and fear-driven family. We were married young and were so different, right from the get-go. I didn't do my due diligence and realized too late that we wanted very different things out of life.

I even accepted that my abuser was a child of God and wasn't innately evil—just lost. He was resonating in guilt and shame. Trapped in a loveless, sexless marriage, he wasn't thinking with his head!

My anger was dissipating.

Each evening, I'd surrender my personal will and ask God what he wanted of me, and every morning I'd wake with a driver so powerful that I felt unstoppable. My life wasn't about just me anymore. There were important things that needed to be done, and I was part of a much bigger plan. As a single mother with no income, I made a bold leap and self-published my first book: a full-color manual with an accompanying journal. In addition, I recorded a seven-CD set called the *Listening Collection* and the *Relaxation Therapy* CD. I also produced *Tight & Toned* (a workout DVD), along with a DVD called *From the Heart . . . Our Stories.*

I spent over $150,000—all on the "promise" of a payback within 90 days. I *literally* had no money; I'd been a stay-at-home mother who'd left with nothing, and my ex-husband refused to pay alimony. I channeled my anger into what I wanted instead of wasting it on fighting him for scraps: I put a plan in place for marketing and distribution, spent countless hours on the phone booking media events and interviews, and eventually felt like I never left my office.

Almost immediately, I landed a spot as a life coach on the nationally syndicated morning show *Canada AM*. Things were beginning to take off! I sent my press kit everywhere and began booking small venues where I could speak to groups of women. Then the magic day came when I was contacted by the president of The Power Within, who asked me to speak at his upcoming event for women, along with Naomi Judd and Joan Borysenko, Ph.D. In a matter of a few months, I went from small speaking gigs in front of 100 to 200 people to an audience of 2,500! I was booked at a few more of their events, hosting and then sharing the stage with Dr. Phil and more than 5,000 in attendance. My books were selling out, and I was pinching myself. Only a few years earlier, I had been a stay-at-home mom, crying about my weight, fighting with my husband, and wondering what I could do . . . constantly feeling trapped and terrified.

I decided I needed to get my books out on a larger scale, so I sent packages (each containing my book, CDs, DVDs, and journal) to two publishing companies: Hay House and Wiley. Both offered me a deal, and I secured a three-book contract with Hay House. Needless to say, the $150,000 I borrowed was easily paid back. For the next four years, I was repeatedly interviewed and appeared on countless TV shows, while hosting my own weekly radio show on **HayHouseRadio.com**®. In 2007, I became the weight-loss expert on the international TV show *X-Weighted*. (The show is in its fourth season, and I'm beginning production on my very *own* TV show!)

On August 8, 2008, I got married in the most beautiful garden wedding to my soul mate—a man with the utmost integrity and authenticity, who loves me for me . . . and a man whom I love just as he is. In a white tent decorated with twinkling lights and flickering candles, white chiffon bustles, white flowers, white tables and chairs, and cascading water fountains, my new husband and I danced under the stars with 100 of our closest friends and family members. I'm the luckiest and happiest woman in the world. Life just keeps getting better.

In January 2009, my 15-year-old half brother moved in with us, and I became his legal guardian. In addition, within a few months we began to open our home to other troubled teens. Let me describe our home: it's filled with musical instruments, and has a basketball court, tennis court, a baseball diamond, playground, pool, trampoline, bonfire pit, and my own "retreat center" . . . all within 50 feet of my front door. People often jokingly refer to my place as the local youth center. I never realized that giving back and loving these kids would fill me with such peace and joy.

I have a good life: beautiful, healthy children; a devoted and loving husband; and four irresistible dogs, three cats (an abandoned litter we took in), and a flock of singing canaries. I live in the most perfect house where I'm able to do what I do. It seems that the more I stop worrying about my career, the more it takes off. I love what I do and am so blessed that it allows me to live such a wonderful life.

Staying in the "City of Love"—letting love be my fuel— takes continual presence, vigilance, and in my personal opinion, the grace of God. I sometimes falter and dip down into anger over things—I'm human. But now I know exactly what I must do in order to channel that anger into courage, a shift that elevates me back into willingness. Then I surrender it to my Maker.

When I completely let go (and that comes *only* after I've done all I can possibly do), I feel peace, a sense of being grounded, and complete detachment from outcome. Through each period of my life, my driver was necessary in moving me to the next state of consciousness, like having the appropriate octane of fuel exactly when I needed it!

❖ ❖ ❖

As you become stronger, happier, and more successful, your drivers will change as well, until finally love will be enough for you to sustain success. But don't worry if your driver doesn't seem that enlightened right now. Similar to stopping at gas stations on a long journey across the country, you'll need to keep refueling to keep going. If your drivers aren't compelling enough, you'll end up running out of gas!

Be honest with yourself: *What drives you right now? Is it enough?* It's time to unleash a fire within you to move you toward empowerment! Start by writing down your drivers in Section 4 of your R_x for Success, and make them big enough for the long and lonely parts of your journey. Be sure to check in with your drivers and adjust them along the way as you become more and more empowered!

5. Your Priorities

Let's get back to your everyday life. You know where you are; you know what your own dreams, values, and drivers are. Now you need to incorporate them and make them a part of your daily priorities.

The most common excuse I hear from people is: "I don't have time. There just aren't enough hours in the day." This isn't true! Of course, many of us feel like the day isn't long enough to accomplish all that we'd like to; however, the real reason we don't fit in our workout, eat a salad, make that really important call, organize our office, create our R_x for Success, make love, face our unfinished business, and so on is because we simply haven't made these things a priority. We're more committed to other stuff—sadly, usually complaints and excuses. We haven't organized our time and created a workable schedule to follow.

Let me paint a picture of how most people manage their time: Grab a blank piece of paper and turn it sideways. Draw three standing rectangular containers; make the two outside canisters the same size and the one in the middle slightly taller. Imagine filling the container on the left with sand. This represents your daily activities. Fill the container on the right with ten rocks. They represent your top-10 priorities. The middle container represents your day.

Visualize yourself pouring the sand (your daily activities) into the middle canister. You'll notice that the sand almost fills it. Now try to put the rocks into the middle canister, too. *You can't!*

It's totally filled up—talking on the phone, returning e-mails, running the kids around, driving to work, watching your favorite TV show, picking up groceries, going to a movie, chatting on social networking sites such as Facebook or Twitter, perusing the Internet, shopping, meeting a friend for lunch, sleeping, cleaning, and even just wasting time on nothing. . . .

Imagine yourself returning the sand and rocks to their original canisters, and you and I will start over together. Let's approach your daily planning differently. Start your day by referencing your ten highest priorities, and place your rocks into the middle container one at the time. For me, one of my ideal workdays (my "rocks") might look like this:

1. Go for a run or practice yoga.

2. Meditate, write, and pray.

3. Eat a nutritious breakfast.

4. Light candles and incense, put on soft music, then return important e-mails and phone calls.

5. Work on my marketing plan, Website, sales strategy, or attend a meeting. (Other days, I'm traveling, filming, or giving talks.)

6. Make a healthy dinner and eat with my family.

7. Spend some quality time with my children and husband.

8. Take a bubble bath.

9. Go to bed early with my husband and read.

10. Cuddle up and *maybe* . . . make love.

Next, take the sand (all of your daily activities), and pour it in the middle container. Because of the open spaces between the rocks, this time, there's enough room for the sand and rocks. *Amazing!* Try actually doing this exercise for yourself, and you'll see that it works!

It's no wonder why successful, confident people always seem to fit it all in and live in harmony. They are very clear about their priorities and always make time for them. They get a lot done in a day because they're organized and focused. If there's time left over for the other things, they'll fit. If not, they'll have to wait for another day.

You'll also find that most empowered people not only work hard, but they also play hard. They understand their balance—the duality that makes everything work properly for them. I'm sure you've heard the saying "All work and no play makes Jack a dull boy." Those who are empowered are *not* dull. But guess what? Empowered people often even "schedule" their playtime! *Without a plan, you plan to fail!*

What are your most important priorities? Are you making time for them? Are you organized? Are you sticking to your plan? If not, what is it costing you? Remember, you can have it all but not all at the same time. Sometimes certain things have to become less of a priority for you in order to achieve a specific goal—this is the fragile balancing act. *If you really want something, it won't manifest unless you make it a priority!*

Take the time to transfer your top-ten priorities into Section 5 of your R_x for Success. Date it.

6. Your Weaknesses

By now you know your values, dreams and desires, drivers, and priorities; but you also know that in the past, you've fallen off track and sabotaged your goals. Why do think that happened? And how can you stop it from happening again?

I bet that if you were completely honest, you could easily state the reasons. You already know your bad habits, excuses, and weaknesses—the things that get in your way of succeeding—but do you have a plan this time to combat them when they reappear? They *will* crop up again!

Like I've said over and over, you need to get honest with yourself. What might get in the way of your success? Close your eyes. What are the first things that come to mind that are weighing you down, holding you back, robbing you of your life force, or clouding your judgment? Be honest and write them all down. The real truth is that your apparent weaknesses aren't really your true weaknesses. What do I mean by that?

Well, it may seem like it's your overindulging, disorganization, procrastination, or big mouth that gets you into trouble and sabotages your efforts, but in truth, it's just the way you've learned to cope in a stressful situation. Your "weaknesses" have given you temporary solace at times. You've held on to them because there's a payoff (even though it's cheap, false, and temporary). Whether it's a toxic relationship that distracts you, a bad habit that numbs you, or an excuse that justifies your behavior, under them is a feeling or a fear that you'd do just about anything to avoid. Your weaknesses are simply a part of the mask you've created to hide behind.

We bandage wounds. *You're still wounded.* You're still in pain, so numbing, distracting, or evading that pain seems like the best thing to do. It's normal and understandable. You may even be surprised by this, because on the surface you don't feel the wound anymore! Your weakness may just seem like a bad habit now. It's both!

So here's what I think: if you spend all of your time worrying about the bandage and not what's causing the wound, you'll never heal—you'll never feel empowered. By focusing on your weakness, rather than understanding what's under it, you're preventing yourself from discovering the truth; and you're robbing yourself of your own power, dignity, and self-respect! And even more concerning is that when you're focused on your weaknesses—always bringing attention to them—you're always beating yourself down. You feel bad about yourself. And when you feel bad about yourself, you can't see who you *really* are. You can't align with your innate gifts, passions, needs, loves, and magnificence. Before long, you're in a terrible pattern of beating up on yourself.

You simply cannot create and sustain success when you feel bad about yourself.

Instead, I'm suggesting that you embrace your weaknesses (okay, maybe not *embrace,* but *admit to and accept*) so that you can heal the underlying issues. (I'll talk more about this in Chapter 5.) For now, just try not to give power to your apparent problems—in other words, stop talking about them, fearing them, or focusing on them. Simply recognize that pain is your spirit's way of showing you where you're not living in alignment with your values, your truth. Your weaknesses are just a way of coping with the lies. The great psychologist Carl Jung wrote: "We cannot change anything unless we accept it. Condemnation does not liberate, it oppresses."

Rather than shame yourself (or anyone else in your life) for making poor choices, be gentle with yourself and simply recognize the feeling you get when you're tempted to fall back into one of your self-sabotaging habits. Maybe you're feeling overwhelmed by something, or perhaps you're afraid, so your weakness is the first thing to rear its ugly head, quickly giving you a convenient way to escape the underlying feeling. "Have a drink!" it whispers to you. "Screw it—go ahead and eat that chocolate bar!"

In plain words: You are at a crossroads! Resistance and suffering are telltale signs that you're avoiding "what is." When you admit the truth about your struggles and let go of judgment, you're elevated above your worries to a place that will channel you to a higher path. (This is what surrendering is!) The secret is that you must be willing to move to a higher manifestation of yourself every time you're suffering. Pain and temptation indicate that you're not where you want to be. In fact, you've lost sight of your values and have strayed from your path—the real reason you're here on this Earth!

In your moment of temptation, why not remind yourself of who you *really* are?

The good news is that temptation is a gift, an opportunity for growth. Your spirit will do whatever it takes to wake you up. Unfortunately, today's world is consumed by immediate gratification and instant pain relief; regardless, you still have an opportunity to make empowered decisions and take the high road.

In his book *The 7 Habits of Highly Effective People,* Stephen Covey writes: "Happiness can be defined, in part at least, as the fruit of the desire and ability to sacrifice what we want *now* for what we want *eventually.*" Life is about making choices. Thank your temptation for showing you that you're feeling powerless, fearful, or inadequate. Then remind yourself that every time you choose to honor your dreams, body, and spirit—by facing the truth of what's really going on—your mind will become clearer, you'll silence your trickster, and you'll grow stronger and more confident.

Power isn't built on a singular life-changing decision: *Should I marry him? Should I take this job?* Power is built on the daily, almost insignificant, decisions! In physics, the equation for *power* is *strength* over *time.* You'll notice that in the beginning, you have, metaphorically, hundreds of crossroads to bear each day. Each time you take the high road, you move farther away from the forest and out toward the hills. You'll soon realize that life has become less complicated; there are fewer hard choices to make. Before you know it, you'll be standing at the top of the hill, looking down upon the millions of people who are scrambling among the trees completely lost. And most important, as you stand at the top of that hill, you feel really good about yourself! You feel proud of yourself. Look at what *you* have accomplished. The only way to sustain success is through loving yourself!

They say it's lonely at the top. I say it's just less congested and much easier to breathe . . . far easier to create and sustain success. Fewer complications! Less drama!

But you should know that getting there—to the top of the hill—isn't always easy, which is what "creation" is all about. Choosing the harder path, for instance, takes courage, but it's the road to freedom. And don't forget that those who are down in the forest don't want to see anyone leaving them. They're like crabs in a bucket: as you try to make a "high road" choice, they'll be snapping at your heels, trying to grab hold of your ankles to pull you back down . . . not because they're mean or evil by nature, but simply because misery loves company.

It takes courage to wake up and make the right choice. It's the brave people who embrace their feelings rather than numb them, feed them, or run from them. It takes strength to face ourselves—the good, the bad, and the ugly. It takes strength to tell the people in our lives how we really feel, what we really want, and who we really are. But the amazing thing about facing a feeling—which creates the craving—is that it, too, shall pass. (And honestly, it will pass quickly, although it may seem like the longest ten minutes of your life.)

If you don't acknowledge the power your weaknesses have had over you in the past, they'll rob you of your long-term values, dreams, and priorities, in lieu of the immediate gratification they bring to you. Besides, whatever pain you don't deal with now will find a way to express itself in your life—also known as addictions!

Life should feel easy and effortless, like floating on a buoy on a beautiful summer day. Instead, most of us live like we're trying to hold the buoy underwater—applying so much resistance is exhausting. There are so many lies that we don't even realize are lies. It takes great effort to live in this way, yet all it takes is letting go . . . of fear, anger, and of the lies we've fed ourselves. We must allow our truth to rise to the surface in order to resonate in our natural and elevated place. Again, try telling this to someone who thinks the buoy is saving her life. Letting go is terrifying!

As you go about your day, be aware of what you're feeling. When a moment of weakness arrives (whether it's making an excuse; complaining and whining; popping a pill; smoking a joint; heading to the bar, mall, or casino; watching a porno; gambling your paycheck; picking up a stranger; working longer and longer hours; or simply vacating in front of the TV all night with ice cream and potato chips) stop and ask yourself, *What am I really feeling?* Don't beat yourself up for the ways you want to escape your fears—instead, look at what's really going on.

Each time you take the high road, your weaknesses lose power over you, and eventually, you'll realize that nothing has a hold on you. *That is true empowerment!*

Take the High Road

Taking the high road may sound easier said than done, but right now, while you're feeling strong and inspired, create the support system you'll need when a moment of weakness arrives. For example, if you tend to eat or drink when you get upset, come up with a list of positive alternatives right now. This will be your line of defense!

Make your arrangements in advance with a person you can call for a talk or walk. Perhaps you could find a workout buddy or running partner. Is there a favorite bookstore you could visit? A journal you could pour your thoughts into (how about visiting our online journal at **www.crystalandrus.com**)? Maybe you could meet up with a squash or tennis buddy to whack away your frustrations together. Could you run a hot bubble bath and meditate? Go for a yoga class? Listen to your favorite playlist? Head to a spa for a massage or manicure? Visit a museum or art gallery to clear your head? You could even just make sure that you have plenty of healthy snacks in the refrigerator.

Maybe you have a tendency to get stressed over your finances and at times pull the covers over your head, leaving the mail to pile up unopened. Or maybe you jump in your car and head to the mall to shop away your woes. You, too, must create your "high road" choices before the next worrisome episode arrives. Call a financial planner now! You don't need to have lots of money to talk with someone. They'll help anyone, even those in dire need of getting out of trouble. Don't be embarrassed! This takes courage, too. Your planner will give you an array of suggestions that will offer you hope and a sense of empowerment. Taking action doesn't cause anxiety; it's the *not* taking action that does!

When your moment of weakness arrives, pull out your "high road" choices, your line of defense, and do something that will add to your life force rather than take from it!

Once you've made your list, read it over every day. Get very familiar with your better options so that when you're faced with a crisis, they become second nature.

The next step is the most crucial one of all: *Before you make any decision—stop! Don't react.*

In order to do so, you must be willing to pause, even if for just 30 seconds (30 seconds of no talking, moving, thinking, speculating, worrying, or considering). Take this time to just breathe and clear your mind. Ask yourself, *What do I want to feel?*

I guarantee you want to feel empowered. You want to create a magnificent life. You want to enjoy the fruits of your labor, not squander them. You want a great relationship, not to get even. You want a beautiful, healthy body, not indigestion and guilt. You want peace, joy, love, and harmony—not fighting, pain, fear, and lack. One road will lead you to your dreams, the other to your downfall. In your moment of weakness, just stop, breathe, and say a prayer:

God, thank you for helping me make the right choice.
Thank you for giving me freedom to choose what I want.
Thank you for giving me so much courage and such a
willing spirit.
There is nothing I can't do through You.

I find that dialoguing with God (or your spirit) throughout the day will keep you on the right path.

Be sure to acknowledge your weaknesses and your "high road" choices in Section 6 of your R$_x$ for Success.

7. Your Commitments

This section is about creating your action plan. *This is so important—in fact, without it, you'll fail.* This step is where you take your priorities and new beliefs (from Chapter 2), along with your values, dreams, and drivers (while also knowing your weaknesses); and commit to specific actions that will move you from your current reality to your envisioned life.

Yes! You must create a daily schedule and follow it! And once your new routine becomes second nature, you need to add *more* commitments to your plan, one by one, and master them as well. Practice is the only way to build good habits. Use the acronym SMART for this goal-setting section: Make Specific commitments that are Measurable, Attainable, and Realistic, with Timelines.

Using the Circle-of-Life Assessment, write down your specific commitments for each area of your life. You may want to jump right into the relationship section, but I want you to begin with your body, then your home, your mind, spirit, finances, and then onto your relationships. It's important that you focus on each area one at a time, until you feel like you're beginning to master it before moving on to the next. It will most likely take you at least 21 days to get each area of your life under control. So follow your commitments every day for 21 days, *not* three days a week! *Every day . . . for 21 days!* (I'll explain more about the synaptic pathways in your brain and how to create lasting habits in Chapter 5.)

Think of it in this way: If it takes 21 days to conquer each of the six areas of your life, that's just 126 days. Imagine feeling like a totally empowered person in four months!

Remember to start with your body, as it's your temple—nothing else in your life will work if your body is clogged and weak. Your body is your conduit of consciousness! If you can't feel, you can't heal. Get your body clear because it's the barometer of your spirit. And when it's clear, you can get your mind to start working the way it was intended—as your navigational tool, not the master of your ship. As soon as you truly feel, you'll begin to hear the whispers of your spirit once again.

Essential fatty acids (EFA) are necessary for proper brain functioning, and if you don't consume the right types of foods, your hormones, including your serotonin levels, won't be balanced. If you don't get enough sleep, your hormones and dopamine levels won't be balanced. Finally, if you don't move your body, your muscles will become unbalanced, and you'll increase your chances of having injuries and strains. You simply can't be a clearheaded, alert, calm, steady person if your systems aren't functioning efficiently.

Here's an example of some goals and commitments for your body (the first area to focus on in your Circle-of-Life Assessment):

Goals	Specific Commitments	Timeline
Lose 10 pounds	I will eliminate fast food and junk food, and eat healthfully.	21 days
Be more energized	I will go on a 20-minute brisk walk 7 days a week.	
Feel healthier	I will drink 8 glasses of water per day.	
Sleep better	I will get 7 hours of uninterrupted sleep each evening (even if it means going to bed earlier!).	
Have more clarity	I will do a 9-day cellular cleanse.	

During the 21 days, you need to regularly check in with yourself to make sure that you're on track. If you're not able to achieve your goals, you may need to uncover any flaws in your plan. *(Perhaps your plan isn't flawed, though—you just aren't following it or haven't given it enough time!)*

Once you feel like you're getting a grasp on your health (keep up with these commitments—doing them should start to feel like second nature), look at your home. Would you describe it as your sanctuary, your haven of comfort and serenity? Is your bathroom a miniature spa retreat, or is it a room that you rush in and out of (and resent cleaning)? How about your bedroom closet? Do you open the door and see your garments hanging beautifully organized, or do you claw through ten years of old clothes in an assortment of sizes? How about that junk drawer in the kitchen? Is it overflowing? Is the laundry hamper filled with mismatched socks? What about your computer? Are your files organized? Do you use it to better your life, or does it consume your evenings with shallow chatting and degrading e-mails? Detoxing is necessary in *all* areas of your life.

When I first began my empowerment journey, I did a major home purge! In fact, I decided to sell everything I owned and start fresh. I'd collected so many things over the years—stuff that I didn't need or even necessary like. I went through my house, selecting certain possessions that were special to me and gathered them up in one room. Then I posted signs around my neighborhood and in the local newspaper announcing an open-house sale. I sold *everything*—from the plates in my cupboards to the art on my walls. The sentimental things were safe, of course, and I was creating space.

I now realize that this action was symbolic of my cleaning out the garbage I'd held on to for so many years. After I initially lost all of my extra weight, I felt so much freer and I knew that I was becoming a different woman. All of the belongings that had once defined me now meant nothing to me. All of those possessions had been distractions, cluttering my space and occupying my mind. As I was shedding the weight, I was ready to discover the woman I was really meant to be.

❖ ❖ ❖

To initially create "Your Commitments" in this success prescription, set aside a full weekend to strategize, as it's not the writing that takes time, it's the planning. After you've created your plan, pick a date to start—*why not this coming Monday?* And then get started! Each evening before you go to bed, write down your seven essential action steps that you must take the next day, and then prioritize the tasks.

After you give yourself time to clean up your body and purge your home, you can trick your trickster; then start doing the tougher stuff: honoring your spirit, facing your finances, and loving with an open and willing heart. The next few chapters will help you with this!

Finally, be sure to create a "Success Tracker," and every three months compare your results with your vision. Are you on track? Are you where you should be at this point? If not, you must be willing to uncover any flaw in your original plan (I'll teach you how in Chapter 8).

Transfer your chart with your goals, commitments, and timelines into Section 7 of your R$_x$ for Success. Keep up the great work!

Chapter Four

ASSUME ACCOUNTABILITY

*"'He insulted me, he cheated me,
he beat me, he robbed me'—
those who are free of resentful thoughts
surely find peace."*

— *Buddha*

*Y*ou simply can't have a ridiculously amazing life until you accept that it *is* your life. If you're not where you want to be, nobody is going to get you there but *you*. Wallowing in misery is pointless. Regretting past choices is pointless. Blaming somebody . . . anybody . . . everybody . . . is also pointless. So is coming up with excuses; focusing on the (perceived) problem; resisting "what is"; and hating your body, job, or spouse.

I don't mean to suggest that you haven't had real setbacks; or that possibly, others haven't abused, hurt, or devastated you. You may have been the victim of extreme violence or neglect. You may have been seriously physically injured, or perhaps someone has robbed you of all your savings. Even in the worst scenario possible, I'll still tell you that in order for you to become empowered, there must be a moment when something inside of you says: *I'm worth more than this!*

If a trauma strikes your family or a disaster destroys your home, of course it's natural to initially feel shaken to the core. You'll grieve and feel sorry for yourself—again, that's natural and normal. You need time for healing. You may feel afraid and vulnerable, and then angry. (That's a good sign! I'd rather you be mad than sad, as anger resonates higher than grief!) But eventually, time passes and you must decide if you're going to get back in the game or remain angry or, worse, a victim.

Bad things happen to good people. Don't beat yourself up over it! Don't convince yourself that you attracted it (although we do have to be careful about what we attract with our thoughts). There's always a bigger plan at work. If you're living in integrity, honoring your needs and the needs of those around you, and something terrible happens, don't own it. Simply accept it and realize that it's not what *happens* to you; it's what you do with what happens that sets your life in motion.

If you've recently been traumatized, only you truly know if you're still in the natural and necessary grieving process. If you are, you have to allow yourself time to heal. But if a voice somewhere inside of you is saying *Enough is enough,* make the courageous decision that you will no longer be a victim of your own life.

No One Is Coming to Save You

Okay, so maybe you don't really think that a knight in shining armor will ride up on his white horse and save you. Unless you're proactively making decisions and taking actions toward creating your dream life, you're waiting for someone to get you where you want to go. I know you've heard all the amazing stories, like the beautiful girl who's "discovered" at a football stadium and becomes a *Playboy* model and famous blonde bombshell; or the one about the homeless mother who finally gets someone to read her manuscript and becomes the number one author in the world. But I'm going to be honest with you: *It ain't never gonna happen to you!* At least, don't count on it.

The good news is that you can save yourself!

You have so many God-given talents and special attributes, but it's up to you to get them out to the world! No one is going to knock on your door and ask to hire you, marry you, or make you the president of their Fortune 500 company.

An empowered person waits for no one to fix her life—but she does wait, at times, for the right moment to take action, and she trusts her intuition to guide her. She knows that as long as she stays true to her dreams and has the courage each day to do *her* part, the Universe, God, the Light, the Divine— whatever you call it—will do *its* part. She's certain that no amount of sitting in the lotus position, meditating on her dreams, or raising her hands to the heavens will bring about success; however, she does know that God helps those who help themselves. God opens doors, but it's up to her to walk through them . . . and you can't do that in a yoga pose!

By assuming complete accountability for all of your actions, lack of actions, and reactions, you'll set your life into motion. You may think accepting accountability, fault, or blame is cowardly or that it will disempower you (by making someone else right), but it actually does the complete opposite. If you're even one percent responsible for why things have gotten off track, accept responsibility and do whatever you can to improve your situation. Who cares about proving yourself right or making someone else wrong! You'll be amazed how your life and the "situation" will turn around (and the ways in which others begin to own up to their parts, too) when you become completely accountable for everything.

Take the following test to see if you're waiting for someone to save you:

Life Jacket, *Please?*

Check the statements that often apply to you. Be completely honest! This is an important exercise to help you figure out your level of consciousness.

❑ I feel embarrassed about the way I look and worry that I will never get better.

❑ Growing up, I never felt good enough, rich enough, thin enough, strong enough, cool enough, pretty enough, smart enough . . . *something* enough.

❑ If only you knew the real me, you'd know I'm not *that* good of a person.

❑ I've been abused—physically, emotionally, verbally, or sexually—and I still harbor those wounds.

❑ I tend to be abusive to others when I feel powerless, but I always feel bad afterward.

❑ I feel like a loser when it comes to saving or making money.

❑ I'm ashamed of parts of my past and have skeletons in my closet.

❑ I'm humiliated by my family or certain members of my family.

❑ I'm tired.

❑ I'm in, or have recently been in, a demeaning and toxic relationship.

❑ I'm always busy.

❏ I have a difficult time saying no—especially to my children or parents.

❏ I feel bad after I speak my mind or get angry.

❏ My health is poor (or I have a chronic disease).

❏ I wish others would notice how much I do.

❏ I often do things out of obligation rather than joy.

❏ I have a difficult time stilling my mind or meditating.

❏ I'm a workaholic or perfectionist.

❏ I frequently feel like I've got the weight of the world on my shoulders.

❏ I'm a people pleaser.

❏ I give up the things I want in order to make others happy.

❏ I feel stuck.

❏ I have little hope that things will get better.

❏ I'm unsure about what lights me up.

❏ I don't know what my dreams are.

❏ I keep attracting situations and people who hurt me or let me down.

❏ I don't trust easily.

❏ I have so much to give but no one to give it to.

❏ I often feel used and taken advantage of.

❏ I wish things were different.

❏ I'm sad about the way things have turned out.

❏ I can't help but remember my past and those who have hurt me.

❏ I've had many friends, many jobs, and many lovers. Where are they now?

❏ Sadly, failure is a big part of my life.

❏ I have a challenging time eating or sleeping.

❏ I struggle with depression.

❏ I've lost my job, my health, or my partner.

❏ I can't get over *it*—him, her, and/or the situation.

❏ I have memories that often keep me from moving forward.

❏ I worry a great deal.

❏ I tend to think ten steps ahead.

❏ I stay in my relationship because I'm afraid of being alone or of what people will think if I leave.

❏ I agonize about money all the time.

❏ I hate my job, but I'm afraid I won't find another one that pays as well.

❏ I exercise excessively because I'm anxious about gaining weight.

❏ I'm scared to spend too much money.

❏ I am controlling.

❏ In relationships, I tend to get jealous easily or fear being cheated on.

❑ I have a wall around me to protect myself from being hurt.

❑ I have an addictive personality.

❑ I tend to compare myself or my life to those on TV or to well-off, attractive people, and I want what they have.

❑ I have all the latest gadgets.

❑ No matter how much money I have, I worry that it's not enough.

❑ I crave attention.

❑ I'm inclined to purchase all the latest fashions and accessories.

❑ I want more than my parents had.

❑ I spend a lot of energy achieving my goals.

❑ I'm competitive.

❑ I don't care if people consider me superficial.

❑ I'm motivated by results.

❑ I feel frustrated much of the time.

❑ I tend to become irritable or explosive when under pressure.

❑ I feel resentful.

❑ I can be demanding.

❑ I can be too reactive.

❑ I'm sensitive.

❑ I hold a lot of anger in and don't know how to express it in a healthy way.

❑ I avoid confrontation.

❑ I don't like egomaniacs or litigious people.

❑ I'm extremely patriotic or religious.

❑ I have a hard time saying "I'm sorry" or "I'm wrong."

❑ I usually *do* know best.

❑ I have strong opinions about many things.

❑ Others would say that I can be argumentative.

❑ If you mess with my family, you're messing with me!

❑ I'm more educated or come from a better family than most.

❑ I feel a sense of entitlement.

❑ I look good and I know it.

❑ I like who I am and don't want to change.

❑ It's my way or the highway!

The list began with statements that reflected lower levels of consciousness—shame and guilt—and then slowly built up into the levels of anger and pride. Although the last 20 were more empowered than the first 20, *all* are disempowered ways of thinking.

A truly empowered woman knows that change is a necessary and fundamental part of success. She also knows that to get something she's never had, she must do something she's never done. She acknowledges that she doesn't know everything and certainly doesn't always need to be right. She embraces the fact that she's completely and utterly accountable for everything in her life. Everything! She realizes that excuses, even justifiable ones, rob her of her dignity and self-respect, and that blaming others or waiting for someone to take notice of how wonderful she is will keep her in the victim mode. There's a big difference between surrendering and giving up, between patience and procrastination, between waiting and avoiding. Where do *you* resonate?

Accountability and Health

When you assume responsibility for your life, you must embrace every aspect of yourself, including your health and well-being. An empowered person can't make positive changes in her career or relationships if she's depressed (and won't seek help) or feels tired all the time (and can't find the motivation to exercise regularly). Remember that no one is coming to save you. Are you ready to take charge of your health? *Let's get started!*

I'm deeply passionate about health and wellness and want to spend some time on this topic, especially on the state of our current health-care system. *Get me going on the topic of pharmaceutical companies and I'd have another whole book—and not a very nice one!* Just take a trip to any clinic in North America, and watch the countless prescriptions being doled out. I promise you that one of the number one ways to disempower your life is to leave your health in the hands of others (especially in the hands of corporate America—billions of dollars are being made from your disempowerment)!

Don't get me wrong: God bless nurses and doctors (especially nurses, who are so underpaid for the difficult and demanding work they do). If you find yourself in an automobile crash or with some acute injury or attack, these are precisely the folks you need. They have the technology and brilliance to save lives. But as far as healing disease—cancer, cardiovascular, diabetes, depression, HIV/AIDS (the list goes on and on)—they simply don't have all the answers. You must take your health back into your own hands. Open your eyes to what you're doing—or not doing—to and for your well-being.

Where the Problem Lies: $ $ $

Cancer, for example, has been unleashing its fury on us, as a nation, for as long as most of us can remember; yet, despite research expenditures now over six billion dollars annually, during the last 30 years, increases in the survivability of the major cancers (including breast cancer, colon cancer, lung cancer, and prostate cancer) can be measured in just a few percentage points.

One must question whether the war on cancer is just *too* profitable to end. And if not, why are we no closer now than we were 30 years ago to finding a cure? I think it's about time that money went into educating the public on the truth: Cancer, along with most diseases, is ravaging us because we're ravaging ourselves—knowingly *and* unknowingly! And most of us are being attacked without realizing it, until it's nearly too late. *It's prevention not early detection that we must focus on.*

Our bodies are overfed yet undernourished. The air we breathe is contaminated with toxins. Our food and beverages are covered in pesticides and filled with hydrogenated fats, sugar, and chemicals. Our meats and dairy products are pumped full of hormones and antibiotics. We spend hours sitting in front of computer monitors, talking on our cell phones, and racing around at a frantic pace, trying to keep up with the Joneses. We pop pills for our constant aches and pains; harbor disappointments, letdowns, and betrayals; and live primarily in the past while worrying about the future.

As I said to my father after he had a mild stroke and was complaining that the medicine wasn't healing him: "Dad, you *don't* have a disease—you have a *lifestyle!* You can't smoke two packs of cigarettes a day, work long hours, eat meat and potatoes every evening, and finish it off with a few whiskey nightcaps and *not* expect it to take its toll on your body. Medicine won't ever cure you! It may mask the symptoms, but unless you change what you're doing, you'll never change your outcome. You can take control of your health, though. It's never too late!"

Wake Up and Smell the Green Tea

More than ever before, we have an abundance of choices; yet sadly, but understandably, especially in our fast-paced and chaotic lives, the quick and easy ones seem to be what too many of us are choosing. It seems that we put more value on the quality of the cars we drive than on the foods we eat. We put more attention on paying off our homes than we do on paying attention to the people in our homes—starting first and foremost with ourselves! We simply have our priorities confused, and in an effort to make life easier, we've totally complicated it.

The body is a perfect example of this: it may be a complex machine with trillions of chemical reactions happening every second, but taking care of it is actually quite simple. As long as we give it what it needs—versus what we *want*—it will run beautifully. Instead, we fill it with foods it can't process, toxins it can't fight, stress it can't tolerate, and medicines that have a crippling result of negative side effects.

And then, we, the weary and scared patient, look to our doctors, hoping they can prescribe us just one more "magic pill" that will save our lives. Sadly, we've allowed ourselves to give away our power and place it on the shoulders of the almighty M.D. Not only does this leave us feeling disempowered, helpless, and afraid, but it also puts all of the responsibility on physicians to *heal us.* And believe it or not, doctors are not actually God! As far as I'm concerned, they carry the burden of this load.

Pharmaceutical companies may be making massive money, but they themselves are filled with employees—regular people just like you and me—who need a better option for their own health, too. It's time to value people more than money. It's time that we value ourselves—our health, our children's health, and the health of this planet!

The good news is that we can not only stop the damaging effects of our current lifestyle, but with a little commitment and willpower, we can actually reverse the damage we've done!

Why not start tonight by going to bed a little earlier and waking up a little earlier? When you wake up, head straight out for a brisk 20-minute walk. Enjoy a breakfast of organic yogurt with a banana, berries, and raw muesli with a hot cup of cancer-fighting green tea. Take a few minutes to give thanks for everything in your life. Take the train to work. Smile. Listen to relaxing music. Have a big salad with salmon or tofu for lunch. Drink plenty of water with lemon. Let your work stay at work as you head out a little earlier than normal. As you walk through the door, kiss your spouse and your kids, and pat your dog. Give thanks again. Do something fun. Turn off the TV. Read a great book. Light some candles. Make love. Clean up your finances. Simplify your life. Meditate. Do a cleanse. Eliminate red meat. Cut back on alcohol. Dance. Sing. Laugh. Live. . . .

It's Your Health . . . Your Life . . . Your Choice!

Although liposuction or gastric-bypass surgery may seem like the easiest way to lose weight (or if finding a rich mate or winning the lottery would be the best answer to your money woes), it's not! If you don't know how you achieved your success, you won't know how to maintain it. You'll always be afraid that you won't be able to keep it up or that someone will come along and steal it. Just think about the woman who loses 20 pounds on a crazy fad diet without exercising and then becomes afraid to eat—terrified that she'll gain it back, obsessively weighing herself every day. Studies show that a large percentage of people who win the lottery are broke within five years, and I can assure you that a rich man's money will always be *his!*

If you don't really know how you created your success and experience a setback (life always gives us setbacks), you'll be an emotional mess, hanging on to whatever scraps you can. On the other hand, if you know how you created your success, you'll have the know-how, plus the jet fuel, to overcome any obstacles and catapult yourself forward again, quickly!

Give Yourself the Good Life

We've all heard the warning that "there's no such thing as something for nothing," and it's the truth. Even when you think you've gotten something for free, if you were to look objectively at what you've traded for that "something," you'll find that there's always an exchange: even in the small things, such as spending money on lottery tickets for 20 years, waiting for lightning to strike rather than using your own intelligence and effort, or giving your name to a telemarketing company in exchange for the chance to win a prize (only to be inundated by phone calls each evening at dinnertime). On a larger scale, perhaps you've given your time, money, family, solidarity, peace of mind, heart, spirit, or even your body in exchange for something. Hopefully, what you gave was worth what you received!

Everything requires an exchange—even misery, fear, and guilt have a cost. Maybe you think that "if it's too good to be true," it is; you've traded off your hopes and dreams, happiness, success, and personal empowerment for the alternative: to live a "not so good" life. But even living a "small life" takes work!

Although get-rich-quick schemes always have a catch— usually demanding that you hand over your integrity, dignity, money, and maybe even your future (should you get caught doing something illegal), I don't believe that everything that's "too good" can't be true. I'm living proof that you can live the good life, but even my life has required bartering. It has required my time, effort, discipline, accountability, persistence, and a plan that I must continually rework. It has required me to face my fears and deal with rejection, betrayal, criticism, and temporary defeat. It has demanded my time—even having to once miss my youngest daughter's birthday! Although living a good life is possible, it didn't come without strings attached . . . but I would never trade it. I've taught my daughters, through my actions, how to be a strong, determined woman. *Children do what they see, not what they hear!*

My dear friend, David Patchell-Evans, who's a self-made millionaire, a five-time Canadian rowing champion, and the owner of close to 200 GoodLife Health Clubs across Canada, has recently written a book called *The Real Sexy, Smart and Strong*. Patch (as his friends call him) would tell you that "life can hit us broadside with things we don't expect. It's a matter of deciding that, no matter what happens, you will be the best you can be."

Patch can personally speak about overcoming hardships while remaining accountable and vigilant to his dreams. Even though he has so much to feel blessed for, he's had his own traumas and setbacks but never lets them hold him back for long! It was Patch, as a matter of fact, who woke me up a few years ago when I was in a debilitating situation, feeling sorry for myself, completely unsure of what to do. The energy it took to be sad and stuck was overwhelming, yet the idea of doing something about it felt even more overwhelming. Nevertheless, as I sat and cried to Patch and shared my woes, he did what a real friend would do: He let me cry for a bit (just to get it out), and then he boldly said, "Crystal, stop being a victim! It's better to die in charge than to die the thousand deaths of a victim. *Charge!*"

At first I couldn't accept what he had to say. In fact, it made me very angry—how dare he call me a victim! *Didn't he know what I'd gone through? What I'd already overcome? How strong and powerful I was? Couldn't he see my pain and suffering? Didn't he understand that I was trying to be an understanding and patient person? How could he be so cold and insensitive?*

After a few days, his words sunk in and I realized that by waiting—by not being accountable for my own life—I was indeed making a choice . . . the choice to be a victim. I had to stop blaming, wishing, and wondering and take complete accountability for my life. Actions spoke louder than words, and I'd heard it all . . . *I'd said it all* . . . and there was nothing left to do except demand more of myself. I was the only one who could give myself the good life! I'd been trading my soul for scraps of love. I was worth more than that!

That day I wrote this mantra:

**To get something you've never had,
you have to do something you've never done.
You must be willing to reach beyond
your comfort zone . . . it's the only way.
What will you do today?**

Later that week, I made the boldest, scariest decision I'd ever made, but strangely, immediately after taking action, a thousand pounds . . . *the thousand deaths I'd been living* . . . were lifted off my shoulders. I felt wildly *alive!* It had been the waiting that had debilitated me! Doing nothing was completely and utterly exhausting. I realized what a terrible trade off I'd been making for so many years. I wanted to sing my newfound courage from the rooftops!

Be Responsible for Your Actions and Reactions

I've given you a lot of examples and told you about my own experiences so you'll understand why it's vital to be accountable for every aspect of your life. How you feel about yourself (and how you feel, generally) and whether or not you create and sustain success in your life is determined by the role you play. If you're willing to take charge, clean up your messes, and reinvent and rebuild as needed, no obstacle in your life is insurmountable. Here are some true success stories and not-so-successful stories of famous (and infamous) people. Remember that no one can sustain success without being accountable for their actions and reactions regardless of their talent, wealth, or influence.

A one-hit wonder is a music-industry term to describe an artist generally known for only one hit single. Think of Bobby Bloom's "Montego Bay" or Sinéad O'Connor's "Nothing Compares 2 U." Why couldn't they sustain success? Was it a lack of talent, focus, or some other cause?

There are also literary one-hit wonders such as Anna Sewell who wrote *Black Beauty,* Margaret Mitchell with *Gone with the Wind,* Emily Brontë's *Wuthering Heights,* or J. D. Salinger's *Catcher in the Rye.* Why on earth couldn't these brilliant writers retain their success and create more than one best-selling novel? Let's look at each of their personal stories:

◆ At the age of 14, Anna Sewell fell while walking home from school in the rain, injuring both her ankles. She was improperly tended to and became crippled for the rest of her life. *Black Beauty* was written during her later years as an invalid confined to her home.

◆ Margaret Mitchell won the Pulitzer Prize in 1937 for her book *Gone with the Wind.* She wrote for her own pleasure and kept the novel secret from her friends.

◆ Emily Brontë was the second eldest of the Brontë sisters. She originally published *Wuthering Heights* under the masculine-sounding pen name Ellis Bell. She caught a chill and, having refused all medical help, died on December 19, 1848, of tuberculosis at the age of 30.

◆ J. D. Salinger is an American author, best known for his 1951 novel *The Catcher in the Rye.* He hasn't published a new work since 1965 and hasn't been interviewed since 1980.

In my opinion, the lack of subsequent success of these authors had nothing to do with a lack of talent or even focus. There were other variables that easily explain their inability to sustain success.

Anna Sewell didn't begin writing until her later years and died before writing another book. Margaret Mitchell lacked the necessary *desire* to publish books. Her second novel *Lost*

Laysen wasn't even found until after her death. Emily Brontë died when she was just 30 years old—the beginning of her writing life. J. D. Salinger's novel caused so much scrutiny that he became a recluse and refused interviews. The controversy clearly scared him.

We can look at the incredibly talented but extremely angry musician Sinéad O'Connor and easily make sense of her fall from grace as well. In 1990, Sinéad's album *I Do Not Want What I Haven't Got,* containing the song "Nothing Compares 2 U" (which was written by Prince), became a massive international hit and spent several weeks as the number one single. The music video also garnered huge accolades. Sinéad was nominated for a few Grammy Awards and won the "Best Alternative Musical Performance Award," but she boycotted the award show.

Her career took a big spiral on October 3, 1992, when the star appeared on *Saturday Night Live.* While singing an a cappella version of Bob Marley's "War" (a performance she'd planned as a protest over the sexual-abuse scandal in the Roman Catholic Church), she held up a picture of Pope John Paul II, tore it up after singing the word *evil,* and roared, "Fight the real enemy!" NBC was immediately inundated with complaints. Her records were destroyed and radio stations refused to play her songs. Since then, she's been trying to recover and recapture her massive mainstream following, but it hasn't happened yet.

Now let's compare this to the commotion caused by the Dixie Chicks in 2003. Just days before President Bush invaded Iraq, lead singer Natalie Maines told a sold-out audience in London, England: "We do not want this war . . . this violence, and we're ashamed that the President of the United States is from Texas" (the Dixie Chicks' home state). The backlash was as bad as that of O'Connor's, with Natalie Maines receiving death threats, their records were burned, concerts were boycotted, and country radio stations refused to play their songs.

Such similar scenarios but with outcomes poles apart. In 2007, the Dixie Chicks came back to win seven Grammy Awards, including "Album of the Year," and then picked up another six Grammys in 2008. As of March 2009, they'd sold over 36 million albums, making them the highest-grossing female band in the U.S.

Why such a different ending—from Sinéad O'Connor's fall into a dark abyss to the phenomenal success of the Dixie Chicks? Again, it had nothing to do with a lack of talent or even focus. The lack of success had to do with other variables that easily explain O'Connor's inability to *sustain* success.

Don't Be a One-Hit Wonder!

As outlined in Part I of this book, we now know that in order to create success, we must first Clean up the mess we've made; Reinvent, rewrite, reprogram, and rebuild our future; Execute a plan; Assume accountability; Take immediate action; and Eliminate negativity. The Dixie Chicks did all these things. They immediately faced the public and began doing as much damage control as possible, saying that although they didn't support the war, they did support the troops. They then went on to redefine themselves and reinvent their style by creating new sounds that would appeal to a different audience—if country-music stations wouldn't play their songs, they'd make new ones for the mainstream stations.

If the Dixie Chicks buried their heads in the sand, cried and blamed others, and became victims who were waiting for their fans to take them back, I don't believe they would have experienced their comeback. Likewise, if they would have remained angry, defensive, evasive, or confrontational, the public would have also rejected them. Instead, these gutsy, courageous women rebuilt their career and waited for no one to come and save them. Their brilliant manager stepped in and helped them map out a precise plan of action. They assumed complete accountability for what they said and the responsibility for rebuilding their group. They went on to eliminate as much negativity as they could by staying committed to each other, their families, their passions, and their dreams. They stayed focused on solutions, while continually uncovering any flaws in their plan. They slowly but surely swayed their fans with dignity, eloquence, and grace; they trusted in the process, asked for help, invested in what truly mattered to them, and never gave up. These ladies took the high road! *When you do that, you are guaranteed success!*

Sinéad O'Connor, on the other hand, took seven years to face her situation. In an interview with an Italian magazine, she blamed her action on "a rebellious girl," and although she asked the Pope for forgiveness, nothing was ever formally sent to the Vatican. Five years after that, she told another interviewer that she wouldn't have changed a thing if she could go back.

Well, no need to worry, Sinéad. Saturday Night Live would never take you back!

Sinéad never took accountability for her actions and never got past the first step in creating an empowered life: *You must clean up the mess—all of your unfinished business.* The rest was predictable. If she would have conducted some damage control (like the Dixie Chicks did), explaining her own personal experience of enduring abuse and her outrage over the sexual-abuse scandal in the Catholic Church, the outcome would have been much different . . . but no one knew her story.

Sinéad's parents separated when she was eight; she claims her mother frequently physically abused her and her siblings. In Ireland, a country that at the time forbade divorce, her father fought to turn over the court's decision to leave the children in their mother's care. By the age of 15, Sinéad, a time bomb just waiting to explode, was in reform school for shoplifting and truancy. She's been quoted in more recent times as saying that during her time at the reform school she "has never—and probably will never—experience such panic and terror and agony over anything."

A few years before the *SNL* incident, Sinéad's mother was killed in a car accident, leaving the angry 19-year-old devastated. Her song "Fire on Babylon" tells about the effects of her own child abuse.

and financially unhealthy, you're romantically unhealthy, too—either in an unhappy, dysfunctional, or indifferent relationship (or not in one at all). How do I know this? Because all of these things are interrelated—they're all about one missing quality: *a lack of personal integrity.* (I know that's a bitter pill to swallow!)

I'm going to break some news to you: no amount of money, dieting, job searching, business planning, or online dating is going to help you fix this problem, because your money woes aren't about money, your weight problems aren't about weight, and your relationship struggles aren't about what you think they're about either. Integrity is the quality or condition of being whole, complete, and undivided. The word *integrity* comes from the Latin root word *integer,* which means "a complete entity"—something most of us aren't!

Yet if you were to ask most people if they had integrity, I'd bet that they would adamantly say yes, because for so many, the meaning of the word has been associated with adhering to a religious or moral code. Perhaps you are righteous and kind or you are willing to serve, so you truly believe that you're living in integrity. Many people compare it to honesty. Although a part of having personal integrity is about being honest, it's about being honest *with yourself*—your wants, needs, feelings, thoughts, hopes, wishes, weaknesses, temptations, dreams, and desires—and having the courage to share your truth and make the changes you need in order to become a whole, complete entity. It's about aligning yourself—your thoughts, words, and actions—*with who you really are, not who you've been or who you fear becoming!*

Sure, maybe you always tell the truth, you pay your taxes, and you're faithful to your spouse, but that doesn't make you a person who is living in integrity. Individuals with integrity have aligned their thoughts, words, and actions with their values. They feel authentic—that is, whole. Those with integrity know who they are, like who they are, and trust themselves in the highest regard.

**If you knew who you *really* are,
you would always treat yourself with respect!
You would be in awe of yourself!**

When we're lacking integrity, we can't commit . . . especially to ourselves! We can't create and sustain success because we don't believe in ourselves, and we don't trust ourselves enough to even take care of ourselves. We don't know what we value most, so we flip and flop like a fish out of water.

Without integrity, we can't set and maintain personal boundaries. We care more about what others think than what *we* think! People take advantage of us because we've taught them how to treat us. In other words, we've taught them to not take us seriously because we don't take our *own* needs seriously! We want to stick to things but don't. Then we beat ourselves up, wishing we weren't so "flaky."

Empowered people, on the other hand, may notice brief periods of time where one area of their lives becomes unbalanced, but for the most part, they resonate in courage and willingness, and will do what it takes to stay committed to their values. They say what they mean and mean what they say. They know what they want, and if they do mess up, they quickly take full accountability, apologize, and rectify the situation.

Everything they think, say, and do is aligned—*at least 90 percent of the time!* If they say they're going to quit smoking, they do. If they say they're going to run a marathon, they do. If they say they're going to love and cherish their spouse till death do them part, they do. *This is integrity.* They keep their word and honor their dreams. They only say yes if they really mean it and have little trouble saying no graciously. Once they make a commitment, they see it through.

People who lack personal integrity aren't consciously deceitful. They may be kind, fun, adventurous, spontaneous, spunky, silly, spiritual, serene, and even brilliant. (But even brilliance doesn't guarantee success.) Disempowered people may have all these wonderful qualities, but they're missing something fundamental: *personal integrity.* They don't mean to let you down or hurt their own kids or their parents. They don't mean to let their bosses down . . . they just can't keep a commitment! They're fabulous at making promises (ones they truly plan to keep), but they can't commit to a diet, a budget, or a demanding schedule in the long term. They're on track, then off. Their "programming" won't allow them to do things differently, even if they desperately want to! And the really sad part is that they hate themselves for it! And what do you know now about sustaining success? If you hate who you are, you'll sabotage because you don't believe you're worth more. You don't believe you deserve a good life.

But just as money problems aren't really about money, commitment problems aren't *really* about commitment. Those who lack integrity want to be successful, but they don't know how to channel their wants, fears, and desires into courage and willingness; they don't know how to get back into integrity! Basically, they don't know how to speak their truth . . . deep down, *they are afraid.*

Maybe this is you?

The Rabbit, the Lion, the Deer, and the Owl

Have you ever noticed that when you've needed money the most, you can't get your hands on it? Or have you loved someone so much that you ended up pushing him away, when all you meant to do was hold him? Everyone has felt vulnerable or afraid at times, but every individual handles pressure in a particular way. When you're in a stressful situation, which of the following are you more likely to do?

- Run away
- Attack the problem head-on
- Become paralyzed by fear and do absolutely nothing
- Patiently plan until the time is right to take action

Let's look at the subconscious mind to better understand this. . . .

The limbic system, located in the center of the brain between the brain stem and the cortex, regulates survival behaviors and emotional expression. It has the task of telling us to eat and reproduce, and holds the instinctive defenses of fight and flight. It has a close relationship with the autonomic nervous system (ANS), which regulates smooth muscles and other viscera: the heart and circulatory system, intestines, bladder, bowel, kidneys, lungs, and pupils. The ANS consists of two branches: the sympathetic nervous system (SNS) and the parasympathetic nervous system (PNS). The SNS is stimulated in states of stress, and the PNS is activated in states of rest and relaxation.

The limbic system responds to threats in part by releasing hormones that tell the body to defend itself, activating the SNS, which prepares the body for fight or flight. When death may be imminent or the threat is prolonged, the limbic system can simultaneously release hormones to activate the PNS, and a state of "freezing" can result—like a mouse playing possum when it's caught by a cat or a frightened bird becoming stiff and seemingly lifeless.

These nervous-system responses—fight, flight, and freeze—are survival reflexes. If the limbic system perceives that there's adequate time for flight, then the body breaks into a run. If it perceives that there's no time to flee but there's adequate strength to defend, then the body will fight. And if there's neither time nor strength for fight or flight and death could be imminent, the body will freeze. Let's compare these different responses to the personalities of four specific animals: the rabbit, lion, deer, and owl.

The rabbit takes no chances. There are too many predators out there, and its instinct, in any stressful situations, is to flee—no questions asked. The rabbit's level of consciousness resonates in fear. In the Chinese zodiac, the rabbit is thought of as loving and selfless but so fearful that it rarely settles down or commits to any one person. Rabbits are worriers, the ones who overthink.

They will avoid confrontation at all costs, even at the sake of their personal integrity. By running away, they hope things will get better, but if they don't, rabbits tend to just sweep the issues under the carpet and carry on, too scared to face the music. They're afraid of failing and of being hurt, so they keep themselves—their lives—small and safe. Rabbits may be the life of the party, but don't count on them when the going gets tough! A rabbit is sweet and lovable . . . but will quickly move on and make new friends or find a new lover along the way. Over time, they feel empty, lonely, and perhaps even a little flaky. Who will take care of and love the rabbit? They've run so many times that they aren't sure how to sustain anything. The future looks scary.

The instinct of the lion is to attack problems head-on: to fight. As an enemy, the lion is a bloody-minded opponent, rarely feeling satisfied unless the threat has been obliterated. Lions attack first then ask questions. Ancient astrologers referred to the sign of Leo as "bestial," meaning reactive to primordial instincts rather than higher reasoning, and "feral" because of their sometimes savage and ferociously vicious behavior. Lions are overpowering; they dominate situations so that they go their way. They like to be in control and leave little to chance, believing that attacking problems is always the answer. They will fight to the end and never give up—their pride won't allow for that! Although much of the time lions are successful—even admired or respected—they annihilate relationships or stunt them before they can ever blossom into something truly magnificent. If you mess with the lion, you'd better be prepared for the consequences.

The deer, when confronted with stress, instinctively freezes—barely breathing. In the wild, when a herd is attacked, there's always at least one who is immobilized with fear and is always the one who is killed. The deer is unsure—and gets, as my brother, Jeff, calls this condition: *paralysis analysis*. The deer doesn't want to screw things up but doesn't trust itself enough to make a decision. The deer doesn't think it's smart enough, strong enough, good enough . . . *something* enough; and is always waiting to get started—waiting until becoming more "qualified" or for someone to come along to tell it what to do. Time is the greatest enemy. Inevitably, the deer becomes a victim of its own life.

Oh, the wise old owls. They know all and see all with their unblinking eyes, perched quietly, persistently focused on their plan. Athena, the Greek goddess of wisdom, had a companion owl on her shoulder who revealed unseen truths to her. It had the ability to light up Athena's blind side, enabling her to speak the whole truth. Owls cannot be fooled, as they always use their keen sense of power and uncanny intuition. Owls take it all in using silent observation, and then make their move at the perfect opportunity. If they happen to miss their mark, they think nothing of it and simply fly silently back to their perches in order to observe and reevaluate the plan. The owl rarely worries, fears little, and lives in the present, knowing that the future is safe. Owls ease into old age with grace, dignity, and knowledge. They are the physical representation of the qualities of trust, ideas, dreams, greatness, and *wings.*

When you're in a stressful situation, what animal are *you* most like? Are you a combination of the first three, rarely knowing the "right" time to act or the "right" way to react?

Avoid the Snake

We don't want to believe that we could ever be the "snake," but the world is filled with snakes. Snakes are those who *slither* into your life, making their moves ever so *slowly* and *seductively.*

Like a cobra who entices his prey with *sultry* moves and a *sexy* demeanor, snakes will *slowly* rob you of your own success, even making it look like they helped you create it in the first place and are doing their best to help you sustain it. But once the money or love is gone (and you feel as if you've had your life *sucked* out of you), the snake will *silently slither* away to *seduce* another unknowing victim.

Become the Owl

The wise owls understand that there is no truth but rather just the way they perceive a situation. They're aware of how they channel their emotions in relation to the situation and rarely make irrational, disempowered choices. Owls know when to fly, when to freeze, and when to attack. They don't assume. They stay detached and present to what is, allowing things to unfold as they should.

Unlike animals, we humans have instincts as well as another part of our subconscious mind that dictates our choices. It's called a "learned response," which can override our natural instinct to fight, flee, or freeze. The only way to activate this is to reprogram our mind to become more like the owl. The reality is a rabbit will always behave like a rabbit, a lion like a lion, and a deer like a deer; but *we* can change the way we behave!

A learned response is an assumption you make based on what you've been taught to believe. It's when you assume a conclusion before an outcome has even occurred; this creates an emotional response within your body. Your emotions create a multitude of biological chemical reactions, including fight, flee, or freeze. This is called programming. (We talked about reprogramming in Chapter 2.)

Sometimes even the most brilliant of us will assume the worst; even though we're right about many things from algebra to chemistry, we're wrong about some potential outcomes. But since our brain believes whatever we tell it, we then create an emotional response and begin reacting from that state—from that "state" of consciousness—and our reality begins to mirror back to us what we expect.

My friend and colleague Candace Pert, Ph.D., the brilliant author of *Molecules of Emotion,* writes:

> Emotions are constantly regulating what we experience as "reality." . . . For example, when the tall European ships first approached the early Native Americans, it was such an "impossible" vision in their reality that their highly filtered

perceptions couldn't register what was happening, and they literally failed to "see" the ships.

Funny, didn't you always believe it was your reality that regulated your emotions and not the other way around?

This groundbreaking information can change the way we look at everything. Since there's no objective reality, problems are only problems if our minds choose to see them that way. This also means that we can create whatever reality we want . . . as long as we accept that we're the programmer.

Dr. Pert goes on to say:

> One extremely important purpose of emotions from an evolutionary perspective is to help us decide what to remember and what to forget: The cavewoman who could remember which cave had the gentle guy who gave her food is more likely to be our foremother than the cavewoman who confused it with the cave that held the killer bear. The emotion of love (or something resembling it) and the emotion of fear would help secure her memories. . . . This is learning.

In a sense, your brain has chosen to remember incidents that it believes will help keep you safe and protected. So if your life isn't the way you want it to be, you must change your perceptions of your past experiences in order to see them through new lenses.

There Is No Truth

Until you embrace that there is no truth, you will continue to make instinctive decisions based on the software programs you began downloading as a child from your parents and not necessarily from an empowered position. Only a select few downloaded the software that instructed an individual to "patiently observe, detach from outcome, and then take appropriate action." Instead, the majority of people were given the downloadable file called *FAIL:*

F: Focus on the problem
A: Assume the worst
I: Insist on being right
L: Look for excuses to justify your situation

As you've already learned, your emotions create your reality, and your emotions came from your beliefs: those of your mother, father, and siblings. Bruce Lipton, Ph.D., author of *The Biology of Belief,* says: "The fundamental behaviors, beliefs, and attitudes we observe in our parents become 'hard-wired' as synaptic pathways in our subconscious minds. Once programmed into the subconscious mind, they control our biology for the rest of our lives . . . unless we can figure out a way to reprogram them."

I compare the synaptic pathways in the brain to a pathway in the forest. When you walk through a forest, you usually follow the same paths. Changing your programming requires that instead of taking the familiar route, you create a new one. Blazing a new trail takes effort and willingness. It requires courage. It requires that 30-second pause that I talked about in Chapter 3. It requires that you stop before you react, stop assuming the worst, stop insisting on being right, and stop looking for excuses to justify your problems or blame others. With your mind clear, ask yourself: *What do I want to feel?* Do you really want to make the situation better or worse? Do you really want to be right, or do you want to feel great? Do you want to get even or get along? You can assume the worst or you can assume the best. It's your choice.

The fascinating thing about your brain is that after only 21 days of "reacting" differently, you'll create a new synaptic pathway, and the old paths will begin to "grow grass" and soon become faintly recognizable. By reacting differently, you shift your biology, creating an altered reality. You release new happy hormones, and soon this more empowered state becomes your norm. Fear is replaced with faith. Anger is replaced with courage. Worry is replaced with wonder. It takes practice, practice, practice—for a minimum of 21 days!

This is crucial information for creating and sustaining success: *You must feel successful before success will manifest in your outer world.*

Feeling successful comes from choosing to align your emotions with empowering feelings. The only way to achieve this is to rewrite your learned beliefs. Learn to look at things through different lenses—the lenses of your spirit. View from a place of trust, faith, patience, acceptance, willingness, courage, and love!

Go back to Chapter 2 and reread it before moving on. Once you do so, allow yourself to briefly look back at all of your past experiences—especially the tough times—through empowered lenses. Could you be wrong about the way you perceived certain events or things in your life? *Possibly?* Yes? Great!

Choose to see your life through these new lenses. Learn from the past. Allow yourself to forgive and live without regrets.

If not—if you aren't wrong about the way you've perceived the past, I implore you to ask yourself: *How can I be so certain? How can I be so sure that things were the way I saw them . . . and that everyone who hurt me* <u>meant</u> *to do so or that every bad thing that happened was intentionally to defeat me? Is there a chance I could have seen things wrong? Is there a chance the "perpetrators" didn't know any better?*

Wouldn't it give you new hope for creating your future if you could let go of your preconceived notions and look at life through more empowering lenses? *Sure it would! But again . . . it's* <u>your</u> *choice!*

If you want extra help with this, sign up for my 21-Day Sustain Success Course offered through The DailyOm (**www.daily om.com**) or through my site (**www.crystalandrus.com**).

The Real Reason You Sabotage Yourself

Some of us were programmed to believe that only "nice" emotions are acceptable and that the not-so-nice ones are bad. We were taught to turn the other cheek, even at the sake of our own integrity. We were told that if we didn't have something nice to say, we shouldn't have said anything at all. Perhaps our parents lacked courage or had low self-esteem, and they were afraid to stand up for themselves, believing that others were better than they were. Maybe they taught us to bury our disappointments, letdowns, and frustrations. Rather than be inappropriate, we were taught to avoid our feelings . . . and run like the rabbit. *Just be nice! Don't make others uncomfortable!* But I bet that even sweet little rabbits feel angry sometimes!

Others were programmed to dry their tears, toughen up, and shut their mouths. Their anger was beaten or bullied into them. As they got older, they discovered that using the same loud voices their parents had used made people take notice. They learned that the same aggressive behavior commanded fear and respect. They've seen people squirm under their command and believe that they must attack before being attacked. Stuck in anger, lions don't realize there's a healthier, more enlightened way to move into the higher realms of consciousness. They may think they're the kings of the castle, but deep down, they fear what will happen if someone tougher comes along.

Or maybe you were someone who grew up being on the receiving end of someone's unhealthy anger and now as an adult, when a situation arises that you view as potentially threatening, you panic and freeze like the deer—unable to make a decision or take action. You've been overpowered so many times that you don't trust yourself anymore. *What if I mess up? What if I make things worse?* Your self-esteem has been smashed into pieces. So you wait and hope something changes. Or conversely, perhaps you had parents who did absolutely nothing when the going got tough. Maybe they nagged and complained, but inevitably stayed in unhappy relationships or dead-end jobs. Or even worse, you had a lion and a deer as parents, and now you're a full-blown victim!

Are you more like the rabbit, running when the going gets tough—too afraid to commit to an idea, person, or dream? Too scared to wait around, take a chance, and trust in the process? Do you leave "them" before they can leave you?

Maybe you're akin to the lion, believing that if you push harder—forcing, persisting, and demanding—you can make things go your way. Do you often destroy or alienate the very things you want?

Or are you similar to the deer: stuck, depressed, and unhappy, missing out on so much? Are you still blaming your parents, husband, ex, boss, or children? Are opportunities passing you by?

Unless you're like the owl, your life—specifically your financial life—most likely resembles one of these three scenarios:

1. You are *not doing* what you love, *not making* enough money, and living beyond your means.

2. You are *doing* what you love, *not making* enough money, and living beyond your means.

3. You are *not doing* what you love, *making* enough money, but are afraid to give up the money because the "means" mean so much.

The secret to empowerment lies in the owl's wise way: creating a plan, trusting the process, staying vigilant and focused, taking calculated risks, and being present while having the patience to allow relationships and business dealings to evolve naturally. The owl is always courageous, keen, insightful, and enduring.

What Are You So Angry About?

Are you angry that you've wasted so many years trying to win people over? Have you put yourself in debt trying to buy people's love and admiration? Are you angry that you've dated people—or worse, had sex with people—you didn't really want to but didn't have the courage to say no? Perhaps you're angry that you've spent years taking a program or course you don't enjoy, or you've adopted a vocation that drains you, just because your parents thought you should? Are you angry about your increasing weight? Angry over your credit-card debt? Angry that no one notices how wonderful you are?

What do you do with all that anger? How have you dealt with it?

Here's something to think about: *If you can't sustain success, you haven't dealt with your anger.* You have unfinished business. Go back to Chapters 1 and 2 so that you can deal with the "stuff" you're in denial over. You haven't processed the pain of your past nor have you discovered empowering ways of coping. There's a great saying: "Whatever is repressed must be expressed." Sabotage is the manifestation of pain and suffering—the manifestation of anger denied. *This is the pain I was talking about in Chapter 3 when we were discussing our "weaknesses."*

I also bet that with so many letdowns, you've begun to give up on the idea of achieving and sustaining success. Maybe you're afraid to fail again: *This could be the final failed attempt that totally destroys me!* Perhaps you're so tired of letting yourself down and disappointing others. You know you're better than this! You really want to lose weight, enjoy amazing health, share a nice home with loved ones, maintain a large bank-account balance, and experience an extraordinary love life . . . but you keep sabotaging. *Why?*

Deborah Cox, Ph.D., Karin Bruckner, and Sally Stabb, Ph.D., the authors of *The Anger Advantage*, write:

> We may believe that if we try hard enough, anger will go away. However, our research shows that anger doesn't disappear; if we try to force it to leave it sneaks back into our lives sooner or later. It may make a grand re-entrance, bigger than ever in a burst of pent-up, explosive raging. It may slither sideways into our relationships, reappearing as criticism or passive-aggressive inaction. It may burrow into our bodies, emerging as a migraine or chronically upset stomach. Anger has a will, and it finds a way to make us listen. Anger is meant to be a part of each of us.

What if, instead of thinking of anger as a negative emotion—as the catalyst for an altercation—you reprogrammed your mind to see it as the necessary fuel needed to raise you from a disempowered place to an empowered position? What if you learned to see anger as an opportunity to make a change that will improve your life or the lives of others? Wouldn't you view anger in a different light? Wouldn't you take action?

A Change Is Gonna Come!

Take a quick look at significant events in history, and you'll see that it was the *channeled* anger of individuals who were able to effect dramatic change despite the opposition.

If we could ask Susan B. Anthony or Elizabeth Cady Stanton, the founders of the women's movement, about anger, I wonder what they'd say. Imagine that just over a hundred years ago, women in America couldn't vote or own property and had no rights over their own bodies. There are still many countries in the world today where it's only channeled anger that will set their women free!

I'd bet that Candy Lightner, the founder of MADD, was beyond angry when her 13-year-old daughter, Cari, was killed by a drunk driver as she walked down a suburban street in California.

And if we could speak to the first African slaves who were brought to Jamestown, Virginia, in 1619, I'd bet rage was what they felt! Imagine—it took almost 200 years for Congress to abolish the international slave trade in 1808, and then another 200 years before a black man was elected as the President of the United States. Nevertheless, *a change has come.*

I had the privilege of dining with Yolanda King, the daughter of Martin Luther King, Jr., before she died in 2007, and I remember her moving words: "Oh . . . a change is gonna come!"

It takes courage to speak out. Yes, our soul wants peace, but not at the cost of our dignity and self-respect. Courage is the manifestation of channeled anger!

Channeled Anger

When I think of the word *courage,* "channeled anger" comes to mind. "Channeled anger" is a powerful force that gives us the fuel we need to shift into higher levels of consciousness. When transmuted, it allows us to move into courage, willingness, and ultimately, love. What most of us don't realize is that anger and frustration aren't necessarily bad things . . . unless we remain stuck there!

In fact, it's only when a person gets angry enough that things change—*they must change!* When I say "angry enough," I'm not referring to blowing your stack, screaming, hitting, or throwing something . . . *that's unhealthy anger.* But haven't you ever been so upset that it forced you to do things differently, to look within and summon the courage to change things, even if you were totally opposed to the change in the beginning?

Haven't you ever looked back and realized that being discontent—being angry—was actually Divine intervention? The amazing Caroline Myss, my fellow Hay House author, says: "Many of our life crises are divinely scheduled to get us to change and head in a different direction."

Anger arrives because somewhere inside of us we know that something isn't quite right. Similar to when we face our weaknesses or temptations, if we allow ourselves to process our anger in healthy ways, it will bring us to the promised land—*empowerment!*

It takes courage to speak your truth, even if no one else gets it. It takes courage to take action; to stop talking about it and just do it. It takes courage to tell the Universe that you're back in the game again; courage to take that leap of faith. It takes courage to be accountable, to step up and make that call, board that plane, or send that résumé. It takes courage—not just to listen to the yearnings of your heart but to do something about it. It takes courage to fly. The beautiful and daring writer Anaïs Nin said: "Life shrinks or expands in proportion to one's courage." Courage is something you can only experience alone.

Kahlil Gibran wrote in *The Prophet:* "The vision of one man lends not its wings to another man." *Success will never come until you take action.* No amount of praying, meditating, or visualizing will get you there.

What Would Courage Have You Do?

The first few times you take the bold and scary step to honor yourself can be unsettling—*okay, even terrifying!* Your hardwiring—your programming—has been taught to emulate the way of the lion, rabbit, or deer. The people in your life will most likely try to convince you to remain as you are. No one likes change and no one wants to feel responsible for the "mess" of someone else's life. But taking your life back with dignity and compassion means letting those in your life "off the hook" . . . *and yes, that's a good thing!*

You never need to demonize someone else or belittle or berate others for why things have gotten so off track. Besides, you're an adult! You've attracted everyone in your life, and you've allowed things to get where they are! Living on the higher road isn't an easy path—in fact, going after your dreams may bring about moments of "perceived failure." There's no guarantee of a perfect life and continued success, but what I will guarantee is that if you don't honor yourself and have the courage to follow your heart, you will absolutely fail.

I find that writing a letter helps me own my "stuff," while at the same time helping me disengage from a potentially disempowering conversation—one with someone who could try to pull me back to where I once was. Here's an example of my courage letter:

Dear _____ *[fill in the blank with the name of the person this letter needs to be written to],*

I'm off track, and I'm going to make some changes. I'm not blaming you—it's not your fault. I've been buying, mortgaging, overextending, eating, cooking, shopping, talking, doing, doing, doing . . . filling, filling, filling . . . and it's caught up with me.

The reason I can't sustain success (why I'm like a roller coaster) is because I'm not even sure what success looks like. I have to figure out what it looks like to me. What I do know is that I can't keep pleasing everyone else while forsaking myself. I can't keep cooking all the meals, eating too much food, spending too much money, and buying too many things—trapped in a job I hate, a home that owns me, and a body that's failing me. I can't keep trying to prove my worth or make you all love me.

Please know that this isn't your fault, even if I've been blaming you for it all. I realize that I've been angry for so long, and I really thought it was about all the things I said it was about: the messy house, the credit-card debt, my weight gain, my poor health, your parents, the kids, my job, blah, blah, blah. *It isn't.* They were all just symptoms of my not having enough integrity to stop long enough to ask myself: *What would courage have me do? What do I really want?*

I've been more committed to being right—to my story, my anger and blame, my wine, junk food, spending, people pleasing, _____ *[fill in your weakness]*; and I've robbed myself of my own dignity, self-respect, and happiness.

I can't . . . no . . . I *won't* do this anymore.

I know that Rome wasn't built in a day and that even the longest journey starts with a single step. Please believe me when I tell you that writing you this letter wasn't easy, but it has taken even more courage for me to admit all of these things.

Thank you for understanding that this isn't about you or the changes that I expect you to make. This is about me: my wants, needs, and desires.

I don't know if everyone (or anyone, for that matter) will understand what I'm going through, but I have to make changes for me, regardless of who "gets it." Once I can trust myself—have complete faith that I'll take care of myself—I know that I'll be able to take better care of everyone else in my life. By doing so, I'll be the happiest, most successful person I can be.

Love,

_____ [sign the letter]

And then why not give it to whomever it's addressed to! We are talking about having courage here!

❖ ❖ ❖

Every morning when you wake up, ask yourself: *What would courage have me do?* Then do it, even if it means that you live "smaller" now but sleep well at night. Invest your efforts into actions that will bring you closer to the big payoff despite the fact that it's scary and you aren't guaranteed a successful outcome. What you will receive is a huge boost of integrity. And when you possess integrity, you resonate at an empowered level of consciousness, attracting the people, places, and experiences that will, *guaranteed,* be the next right step in your journey. Ultimately, success will be yours!

The World Doesn't Pay You for What You Know— It Pays You for What You Do

No matter how smart you are or how many Ph.D.'s you have, if you don't take action you won't accomplish anything! Successful people are highly action oriented. They simply get up and do what has to be done. Once they've developed their plan, they get into motion. Even if they don't do everything right, they learn from their mistakes, make the necessary corrections, and keep progressing, all the while building momentum, until they finally produce the result they set out to achieve!

Chapter Six

Eliminate Negativity

*"In minds crammed with thoughts,
organs clogged with toxins, and bodies stiffened with neglect,
there is just no space for anything else."*

— *Alison Rose Levy*

or years, we've been told to "let the sun shine in" and "face it with a grin," and that "winners never lose, and losers never win"; but many of us are still a little cynical and question the notion that our attitudes really do have the power to dramatically influence the outcome of a situation. Nevertheless, science tells us that we—our thoughts, emotions, and actions—create our reality. We aren't innocent bystanders in our own lives, no matter how much we may want to believe that we are.

Maybe you're wondering about the same things that I did when I first realized this! For example:

◆ *How can the thoughts I think, the words I speak, and the actions I take transform a potentially negative outcome into a positive one?*

◆ *How can I change my destiny?*

◆ *How can I alone create riches and great health or find everlasting love?*

◆ *How could I possibly have this much power?*

Let Your Light Shine

Science has proven that you are pure light . . . *energy and power.* Yes, it's true! You may not know this, but everything in your body from your blood, skin, and organs are composed of atoms. That's right! You're made up of subatomic particles— bundles of vibrating energy—all moving at various speeds. And to top it off: *they are 99.99999999 percent empty.*

This is so important to understand: *Although you appear to be a physical being with bones, organs, hair, and so forth, you are, in fact, millions of different "packets" of vibrating energy.* The reason why you "see" your body parts differently (even though they're all of the same vibrating energy) is because your "energy-processing eyes" translate these frequencies into different molecules, shapes, and organs.

Actually, everything in the universe is composed of this same vibrating energy that's moving at various frequencies and intensities. The difference in vibrational output is what makes things appear as different forms or physical manifestations. This means that we're all from the same "field of energy" or "field of consciousness" . . . or what I like to refer to as God.

Since you came from God, you possess the same potential energy, or power, as God does—should you choose to resonate at the highest frequencies. This is why I stress the importance of knowing who you really are!

Knowing this, we also see that our emotions are energy; and our thoughts, possessions, and even the foods we eat are energy. Music is energy, vibrating at a frequency that our "energy-processing ears" translate into specific sounds. Words are energy. In his book *The Hidden Messages in Water*, for example, Dr. Masaru Emoto explains how he captured images of changes to the molecules in water. Water that was literally spoken to with love and kindness responded by forming incredibly beautiful crystals, whereas water that was subjected to hateful words or had come from war-torn areas had distorted shapes, with no sparkle or shine. We must wonder: *Is it really the words that were used or the vibration that each word resonated at that transformed the crystals in the water?*

Albert Einstein said: "Energy is never lost—only trans-ferred." If our choice of words can change the energy in water, imagine how much we affect each other by the things we say!

One of my favorite movies, *The Matrix*, compares a human being to a battery—one that can power an entire city block. Science tells us that we have over a trillion cells in our bodies, each with the capacity to deliver 1.17 volts of electrical power. That would mean that we have, within our control, at least a trillion volts of power . . . should we want to draw upon it! The more energy we have, the more power we have.

The more power you have, the more light you shine! You can unknowingly emit a huge, beautiful aura that surrounds your physical body. Imagine lighting up an entire city block! You can feel amazing, look extraordinary, and notice that people are naturally drawn to you. I go into great depth explaining how to achieve this magnificence in my book *Transcendent Beauty*. For now, just know that your level of "power"—your resonance—is your choice, and it's within *your* control!

Most people are unaware that the thoughts they think, the words they speak, the food they eat, the music they lis-ten to, the people they surround themselves with, the space they live in, and the amount of exercise they get affect how empowered they feel and how much "power" they possess. In fact, here are some fascinating statistics: there are 81 watts waiting to be harvested from a person sleeping, 128 watts from someone standing at ease, 163 watts from a person walking, 407 watts from a briskly walking person, 1,048 watts from a long-distance runner, and 1,630 watts from a sprinter.

Can you see that someone who is physically fit is simply more powerful than someone who isn't? *Exercise is crucial in eliminating negativity and sustaining success.* You simply have more energy and stamina to see things through . . . and the fact that you'll also have thinner thighs is a bonus!

Develop Magnetism!

The magnetism I'm talking about is the kind that draws people in, and without warning or effort, they're magically under your spell. Business meetings go off without a hitch, friends love to be around you, and your mother-in-law wishes you were "her own flesh and blood"!

On the other hand, you've probably been around people who swear they know you; however, you have no idea who they are. These are the individuals who are "present" but have *no* presence!

Magnetism is all about personality! It's about being a good conversationalist as well as a good listener. Those with magnetism have a great sense of humor, a lively imagination, a pleasing tone of voice, a warm smile, good facial expressions, and a large vocabulary. Magnetic people are hopeful, ambitious, and have high expectations. They have and show "class"; they're sharp dressers, cheerful, confident, creative, energetic, optimistic, outgoing, playful, positive, spontaneous, and witty.

You can have the perfect body, perfect car, and perfect pocketbook, but without personality, you'll never be remembered!

Andrew Carnegie, one of the richest men in American history, rated "a pleasing personality" at the head of the list of qualifications for success and went so far as to say: "Personality could often be substituted for brains."

Putting the Law of Attraction in Its Place!

If I read one more book about the Law of Attraction, I think I might scream! We've all been inundated recently with this "law," so I must share my thoughts on it quickly and simply. . . .

The term *Law of Attraction,* although used widely by today's New Thought writers, has a variety of definitions. More than a hundred years ago, it was used in relation to physics and how matter and physical structures develop. A more modern agreement is that the Law of Attraction, based on the same fundamental discoveries in physics, states that people's thoughts (both conscious and unconscious) dictate the reality of their lives whether or not they're aware of it: "like vibrations" are attracted to each other, while dissimilar ones repel each other.

In other words, if you want success, you must think successfully and feel successful, even if you're not yet. (That's the tricky part for most of us!) Remember the crucial information I gave you in Chapter 5: *You must feel successful before success will manifest in your outer world!*

Some scientists say this new definition of the law is questionable: although brain waves do have an electrical signal, any magnetic field produced by the brain is actually negligible. One thing we can all agree on is that scientists are never unanimous in their opinions of almost any topic, whether it's history, economics, religion, metaphysics, or political science.

What I do know is that "birds of a feather flock together"—whether it's because of familiarity or a universal law in action, I'm not sure . . . and frankly, I don't really care. I know that I'm attracted to people who are positive, success driven, honest, real, and spiritual—people who are just like me! Perhaps it isn't just "brain waves" that I'm feeling from them; maybe it's because their bodies are producing energy and their magnetic fields (their auras) are so warm and inviting . . . so beautiful and powerful! (Auras are real and can be seen by the naked eye.)

Remember that every cell has the potential to produce 1.17 volts of energy. Happy emotions resonate faster and are, therefore, more powerful than sad emotions. Many body-mind scientists believe that emotions aren't just felt in the brain but in the entire body—in every cell of the body; this would mean that we're exuding a lot of magnetic energy!

When I've been at the lowest points in my life, I seemed to attract those who affirmed that I was in a low place. When we were together, we could really spin each other into a depressed tizzy: "Woe is us!" But when I feel amazing, I attract situations and people who affirm that I'm clearly on track. When I'm with positive people, I feel their power. Together we're like a ball of blazing fire. I've been out with empowered friends and when we walk into a place, we bring the roof down! (And it's not our "looks"—people feel our presence. It's obvious!)

I believe in the Law of Attraction; however, I think that positive thinking is only *one part* of creating and sustaining success—as you can see with *all* the steps outlined in this book! You can't just "think" and "attract" your way to empowerment. Besides, the fact remains that you aren't always going to attract wonderful events into your life. To suggest otherwise is *simply . . . wrong!*

No matter how great your life is or how positive you are, at some point, you'll experience difficult events, such as the death of someone you love, financial strain during a recession, or the loss of your home in a natural disaster. I think that living solely by the Law of Attraction can cause disempowered people to feel even worse—guilty or even responsible for creating their own illnesses or traumas. As I mentioned earlier, remember that *bad things happen to good people.* So don't beat yourself up if something rotten has happened to you. To recover from a bad situation, you must change the way you look at it. It's done and behind you. You must move on, and if you can't, you must channel your anger into courage, channel your sorrow into strength, and get your life back on track. Sometimes you simply have no choice but to totally reinvent your life . . . because everything you once believed or hoped for has been destroyed. You must rebuild your inner power and increase your personal resonance.

The Law of Resonance is actually another "universal law" that I totally adhere to! It states that when two energies are within close enough proximity to one another, their intrinsic energies come together causing one of two things:

1. **Phase Summation:** Also referred to as "in accord with," as in "striking a chord with"

2. **Phase Cancellation:** Also referred to as "not in accord with," as in "killing my vibe"

We've all been around people with whom we have "phase summation"—we just hit it off and, synergistically, create magic. Conversely, we've also encountered that person who takes the wind out of our empowered sails! (We'll talk more about phase cancellation a bit farther along in the chapter in the section called "Eliminate Toxic Relationships.")

❖ ❖ ❖

Here are other scientific discoveries you can use to eliminate negativity so that you can *create* and *sustain* success:

◆   You control your personal resonance using the
    thoughts you think, the words you speak, the
    food you eat, your surroundings, and exercise.

♦ You'll never feel powerful in a low-resonating temple. Treat your body well.

♦ If your internal radio is set at station 98.1, you can't hear the music being played on 107.1. You must set your internal dial to receive what you want!

♦ There is no objective reality—your emotions regulate your reality. But just as an emotional response can change, the receptors in your brain that sense each emotion can change in their level of sensitivity. This means that even when you're "stuck" emotionally, fixated on a version of reality that isn't serving you, you can change your biology. You *can* reprogram yourself!

♦ Our mood affects our performance. When you feel good, you perform better! Not to mention when you feel good, you'll see the good in others and have more loving thoughts toward them. You'll easily find a solution for a problem if you're not set at the "emotion of fear."

♦ Our mood affects our memory. If someone you love hurts you enough times, you'll learn to feel threatened in their presence and act accordingly— another facet of programming. When you feel sad, you focus on and remember your tough times. When you feel good, you tend to remember good times!

♦ You can only see things that you're willing to see, and you can only find things that you believe you will find. The mind isn't capable of taking in everything it sees and will scan its outer world for objects that it's prepared to find. If you're open-minded, the future is limitless!

The Conduit of Consciousness

If there's no objective reality (nothing is "real") unless you give it power, then all the drama, arguing, pain, trauma, anger, sadness, depression, and even physical sickness is *not* real. At least it doesn't have to be. You've created it and made it real. This also means you can stop creating it and start creating success!

Imagine for a minute (and this takes an open mind) that all of your problems are just illusions, distracting you from the real "stuff"—such as discovering your life's purpose, loving others, evolving consciously, making a difference, giving and receiving joy, and helping others wake up to their purpose. I've even gone so far as to imagine that perhaps the world is like a holographic image, much like the film *The Matrix* depicts. (Okay . . . stay with me and *really* expand your mind!)

Imagine this: What if most of the world is still asleep? What if there are billions of people just going through the motions? What if all the distractions that they get caught up in are actually designed to keep them so busy (also known as "sleeping") that they never wake up to what they're really here to do? What a loss of light! And if something isn't light, it's dark; therefore, if someone isn't light, he or she is dark. . . .

I believe the world is filled with six types of people:

1. Those who are still asleep—still in the dark

2. Those who are beginning to wake up

3. Those who are awake (light workers) and shine their bright light to help others wake up

4. Those who help light workers do their job (light protectors)

5. Those who are amazing "networkers," who connect different light workers to synergistically do incredible work in the world (light connectors)

6. Those who try to put out others' light and keep people asleep (evil)

This isn't the book for me to get into too much depth about my thoughts on light workers, light connectors, and light protectors, but I've always believed that those who are empowered and enlightened are *Earth angels*. They are successful, a joy to be around, and so powerful that they effortlessly bring others out of their sleep and wake them up to their own magnificent light! What if we all woke up one day and took back our light? If we all drew on our maximum capacity of potential electrical power, maybe there would be no darkness in the world. Perhaps this is what heaven is.

I know this concept may not be aligned with many people's idea of success; maybe it even seems sort of "woo-woo," but I know that we all have a purpose, a reason for being here. And it's not to lie around playing video games, reading tabloid magazines, watching pornography, or fighting with our children. It can't be! Yet sadly, most of us have gotten so sidetracked— distracted by all the "garbage"—that we end up living fake and shallow lives. We become inauthentic, and we never wake up to our potential!

If you believe that all the other stuff that wastes your time and robs you of your dignity is real, then it will become your truth. You'll actually believe your own lies . . . your weaknesses . . . your story. You'll give power to your sicknesses, syndromes, and dysfunctions. You'll get caught up in the drama. You'll crave your addictions and justify your excuses. And it will all feel real—just as real as a vivid dream when you're *sound asleep!* It's time to wake up to your potential. Wake up to why you're really here. The starting place is within your body. . . .

Your body is your vehicle for being—your barometer of truth. When your body is resonating at a pure and high frequency, it can identify truth effortlessly. It's clear because *you* are clear. Your body feels a lie immediately, right in the pit of your stomach. The minute you get off track, or when you do something that's out of alignment with your values, you instantly feel it.

But when your "vehicle" gets clogged, burdened, over-worked, and undernurtured, it can't feel truth with the same accuracy. You get tired easily. You have a hard time making decisions—or at least, making decisions with absolute certainty. When you body is "plugged" you can't plug in to the highest levels of pure consciousness. *Why?* Because you attract from where you are! If you're resonating at a low place, you can't attract high vibrational energy. You'll never feel empowered in a low-resonating temple. Instead, you just want to sleep, and like a rechargeable battery, plug back into some kind of "universal power." (This is the reason why we sleep at night and also why depression causes people to sleep more.)

Eliminating negativity is crucial for you to be able to become a conduit of pure consciousness. This goes back to cleaning things up. . . .

Eliminate Toxins in Your Body

Originally designed to be perfectly operating machines, our bodies have become "sick" with the toxins we've been feeding them for generations. Once self-healing, we've begun to turn on ourselves. We've taken so much medicine that we've become immune. We've eaten so many preservatives, additives, food coloring, chemicals, and "bad" fats (the list goes on and on), that our bodies are shutting down—*clogged.* We have diseases now that no one even knew existed 50 years ago.

We pop something in our mouths to go to sleep at night and drink coffee to wake up in the morning. We get our sugar highs through the day to keep us going and overindulge in heavy meals or non-nutritious, empty calories just before bed. Because of this lifestyle, our bodies—our temples—can no lon-ger filter properly. Even our children are being born already sick from the years of damage we've done to our DNA. God hasn't done this to us . . . *we* have.

In the beginning, we were made perfect—in God's own likeness. But with our own free will, we've eaten what we've wanted, cooked how we've wanted, and allowed government and big business to contaminate and genetically modify our foods for bigger profits. Most of the so-called natural foods we're eating aren't even real anymore! Meats and dairy products are filled with hormones and antibiotics. Little girls are getting their periods younger than ever. ADHD, fibromyalgia, diabetes, depression, autism, cancer, and epidemic levels of obesity are rampant! We have a generation of children who are predicted to live a shorter life span than their parents. We have to realize that we've been placing more value on the cars we drive than on the foods we eat. It's our greatest downfall—nationally and globally.

We send bags of grain to starving people in developing countries rather than give them simple packets of "nutritionally engineered food" that could save their lives. I'm reminded of the movie *The Matrix* and smile each day as I enjoy my perfectly formulated protein shake that has just the right amount of essential amino acids, essential fatty acids, and low-glycemic carbohydrates.

Imagine if we'd simply send a plastic shaker cup and enough packets of this perfectly engineered powder to every mother in undernourished countries. As long as she had healthy drinking water, she wouldn't even need electricity to help her family become self-healing machines. Once their bodies are resonating in a higher, healthier place, we can educate them—then we can motivate them! Starvation—whether in our country or abroad—is the work of evil. Bodies become so weak that their light is almost snuffed out. This is our greatest travesty as human beings, and there's no reason for it. Shame on all of us!

You owe it to yourself and to those you love (especially since you live in a country that provides you with an abundance of healthy organic food) to treat your body with respect, dignity, and reverence. When you take care of your body, it will take care of you. This is the first and most crucial step to living a long, empowered life!

Cleanse Your Body

Did you know that the average 24-year-old has from 5 to 15 pounds of mucus lining the small intestines from all the toxins ingested? This mucus is now blocking good and bad food from entering the body's system. The brain isn't getting the essential fatty acids (EFAs) it needs to do its job (much like a vehicle going without oil), and hormones become out of whack. Many people may begin feeling down and believe it's full-blown depression, when it's actually caused by a void in the nutrients that their bodies and souls require. *Talk about a chemically imbalanced culture!*

Doing a proper cellular cleanse will increase your energy and vitality, give you clarity (it's cleansing *all* the cells in your body, including your brain!), reduce cravings, and release excess body fat.

If you want more information on cleansing your body or eating a high-bioenergetic diet, visit me at **www.crystalandrus.com**.

Eliminate Toxins in Your Environment

There's no argument that we have more toxins in our environment than ever before, and in a 2006 article published in the *Toronto Star:* "Researchers suspect these toxic chemicals have links to a number of cancers, including breast, testicular and non-Hodgkin's lymphoma, not to mention reproductive disorders and learning disabilities."

In a study conducted by the watchdog group Environmental Defence, volunteer Sarah Winterton, a program director and mother of three teenagers, found out that she had 16 respiratory and 38 reproductive toxins, 19 hormone-disrupting chemicals, and 27 carcinogens in her body. The tests also revealed traces of lead, arsenic, and uranium, as well as chemicals found in pesticides, flame retardants, and stain repellents in her system. "There are likely thousands more chemicals in me," Winterton told the *Toronto Star*. "It's not a great picture to have of yourself." Not surprisingly, studies conducted on volunteers in the United States and Europe revealed similar findings.

A report published by the Environmental Working Group, a nonprofit research organization, took blood samples from the umbilical cords of ten newborns to test whether they were exposed to particular toxins while in utero:

> Researchers found a total of 287 chemicals from the entire group including two chemicals that were banned in the 1970s and other chemicals used in gasoline, garbage treatment, power plants, the production of flame-resistant products, plastics, Teflon, and wood preservatives. Some of these chemicals have been linked to cancer, endocrine disruption, and neurological impairment.

Is anyone safe from toxic chemicals? The answer is *no!*

Although the American Chemistry Council claims to make products that "help keep you safe and healthy," consumers are actually exposed to myriad chemicals and additives embedded in toys, cosmetics, plastic water bottles, and countless other products.

Did you know that the cosmetics industry in the United States is largely unregulated? According to an article published in the *San Francisco Chronicle* in February 2009:

> The Campaign for Safe Cosmetics [CSC] lists numerous toxins that appear regularly in cosmetics and personal-care products, among them lead and phthalates. Phthalates are linked to birth defects, including disruption of genital development in boys, decreased sperm counts and infertility. Lead appears in lipstick and hundreds of other products. The CSC reports that "lead . . . is a proven neurotoxin—linked to learning, language and behavioral problems . . . miscarriage, reduced fertility in both men and women, hormonal changes, menstrual irregularities and delays in puberty onset in girls." This is the stuff women and girls are putting on their lips all day, licking it off and reapplying.

Are you waking up to this?

For example, the synthetic candles you burn in your home, the colored polish you apply to your nails, the tuna eaten from a tin can, the scented lotion absorbed into your skin, and your nonstick cookware contain chemicals that have been shown to cause illnesses and diseases ranging from organ damage to cancer in laboratory tests. Your microwave, plastic wrap, plastic bowls, and water bottles (which are transported to grocery stores in trucks that get very hot or very cold) may leach toxins into your food and water. Carpets, upholstered furniture, mattresses, and even the plastic casings around your computer and TV all contain flame retardants, which emit polybrominated diphenylethers (PBDEs) into the air. And those are just the toxins in your home!

The documentary *Chasing the Cancer Answer* tells us that nearly 31 million pounds of carcinogens are released into the atmosphere in Canada each year, childhood cancer is up 25 percent in the last 30 years, and breast-cancer rates have increased 54 percent over the past 26 years, even though billions of dollars have been spent on research. *And that's only Canada!* To learn how many toxins are released in specific cities and states in the United States, go to **www.epa.gov/tri/**.

The Toxics Release Inventory (TRI) Program (which was created by the EPA) is a database containing detailed information on nearly 650 chemicals and chemical categories that approximately 22,000 industrial and U.S. federal facilities manage. According to the TRI Public Data Site, of the 21,996 facilities who reported to the TRI in 2007, more than four billion pounds of toxic chemicals were disposed of. *Big business is resisting the cleanup that <u>must</u> happen in order to create and sustain an empowered future!*

This is no different than creating any other type of success, and we must do our part to Clean up the mess that's been made! We must demand that companies Reinvent and rebuild cleaner, healthier products and that our political leaders Execute a plan of action. Companies must be held Accountable. Now is the time to Take immediate action to Eliminate negativity!

Our children depend on us to *create* a new world—one that they can *sustain!* We, as individuals, must do our parts to minimize our impact on the environment (and ourselves) by going green! (You also owe it to yourself, and to our world, to watch Al Gore's documentary *An Inconvenient Truth.* It's life changing!)

Here are 10 easy things you can do at home to begin making a change:

1. *Get a water filter.* Not only are we destroying our world by piling mounds of garbage and tons of empty water bottles into landfills, but most people are unaware that many companies that produce bottled water are largely unregulated. In fact, many major bottled-water manufacturers start with municipal tap water! In addition, some studies have shown that bottled water can contain more harmful bacteria than tap water.

2. *Compost.* By composting you can reduce your household garbage by about one-third. Imagine if all industrialized nations demanded that its citizens compost? If you have the luxury of living in an area that picks up your compost weekly, there is no excuse. If you don't, however, contact your municipality to purchase your own unit. Not to mention, your compost will give your garden some glorious fertilizer—*for free!*

3. *Use reusable grocery bags.* Did you know that plastic bags are nonbiodegradable and can sit in landfills for up to 1,000 years? Plus, using reusable grocery bags means less plastic bags manufactured, which in turn lowers greenhouse-gas emissions. This is a very simple yet effective way of saving our earth!

4. *Use eco-friendly cleaning products.* The long list of chemicals used in conventional-cleaning products may kill germs, but they pose distinct hazards to our health. The dangers are sometimes immediate—as in the case of burns to the skin or respiratory or eye irritation—but over time, they can cause cancer and other deadly diseases.

5. *Don't microwave plastics.* Study after study has shown that putting *any type of plastic* into your microwave will cause the chemical bisphenol A (BPA) to leach into your food. You can't see this happening, nor can you taste it or smell it. But many scientists believe that BPA is "one of the major chemical time bombs of our era," causing a slew of health problems (particularly reproductive) in both men and women.

6. *Use energy-saving bulbs.* We often don't realize how small things like switching to energy-saving bulbs can help the environment, and yet, if every American home replaced one regular lightbulb with an energy-saving one, pollution would be reduced by the equivalent of one million cars driving in the U.S.! Plus, we will reduce our own electricity bills, and these longer-lasting bulbs will reduce waste in landfills. All good stuff for the world!

7. *Recycle smart.* One man's trash is another man's treasure! Before dropping off your unwanted or unneeded furniture, electronics, cell phones, appliances, clothes, and even shoes at the dump, consider recycling them. For example, Nike's Reuse-A-Shoe program grinds up old sneakers into playing surfaces like basketball courts. One World Running collects donated shoes and sends them to athletes in developing countries. The organization Dress for Success provides donated professional clothing to low-income women entering the job market. Check your local area for recycling programs. Many of them will come right to your door to pick up your "junk."

8. *Trade in the clunker.* According to Earth911: "1995 model year and older vehicles produce 19 times more smog-forming pollutants than 2004 and newer models." Vehicle emissions have a terrible impact on the environment. To make an even bigger splash, consider getting a hybrid car, and why not ride your bike to work? Not only are you helping to save the world, you're saving yourself!

9. *Pay attention to packaging.* We have become a world where "bigger is better," and sadly yet unnecessarily, the average American produces about four-and-a-half pounds of garbage each and every day—most of it on needless packaging, cardboard, and plastic! Before buying your favorite item, consider the cost it has to the environment. The only way to teach corporate America is to hurt their pocketbooks.

10. *Become a "flexitarian" (or even better, a vegetarian!).* In 2008, there were approximately 6.5 billion people on Earth, and this number is expected to rise to 9 billion by 2050. As the world's population continues to grow, our requirement for food will also increase, and massive amounts of grain and soybeans are grown to feed farmed animals. Remarkably, 1.4 billion people could be fed with the grain and soybeans that are fed to U.S. cattle alone! The Environmental Defense Fund estimates:

> If every American skipped one meal of chicken per week and substituted vegetables and grains . . . the carbon dioxide savings would be the same as taking more than half a million cars off of U.S. roads. . . . If every American had one meat-free meal per week, it would be the same as taking more than 5 million cars off our roads. Having one meat-free day per week would be the same as taking 8 million cars off American roads.

If you won't give up meat completely, consider cutting back substantially. Not only is it bad for the environment, it isn't good for your body either!

Five Eco-Labels You Can Trust

 USDA Organic labeling means that food is produced without antibiotics, genetic engineering, or most synthetic fertilizers and pesticides.

Rainforest Alliance Certified means that companies harvesting the food practice soil and water conservation; they also reduce the use of pesticides. This labeling is seen on coffee, chocolate, and bananas.

 Fair Trade Certified means the food is grown on small farms and farmers receive a fair price. You'll often see this on coffee, tea, chocolate, fruit, rice, and sugar.

 Certified Humane means that any animal that has been raised for dairy, meat, or poultry has been treated humanely. Growth hormones are prohibited and animals have been raised on a diet without antibiotics. You'll often see this label on eggs and meat.

 Green Seal means that the product has been evaluated for environmental impact. They must meet recycling and bleaching standards. You'll see this on napkins, paper towels, and toilet paper.

Excerpted from Leslie Billera, "Easy Ways to Go Green," *Good Housekeeping.* **www.goodhousekeeping.com.**

Eliminate Toxic Relationships—*Ouch!*

Ah . . . relationships! This is the part of life that hurts and helps you the most! Because people emit so much energy (even a low-resonating person), those with whom you choose to spend your time have the biggest external influence on your success—more than any other factor. Their emotions influence your emotions; their success influences your success. And the more time you spend with certain individuals, the more alike you'll become! This reminds me of the well-known saying: "Show me your friends and I'll tell you who you are."

You also have to know that the people in your life are there because you attracted them: "When the student is ready, the teacher appears." We are all teachers and students to each other; sometimes we learn the greatest lessons from the most *un*obvious teachers.

Whether due to the old "birds of a feather flock together" cliché or the Law of Attraction, the people in your life are there for a reason—or at least, they *were* in your life for a reason! You have to decide if you should still be spending time with specific individuals. Have you learned what you needed to learn yet? Are they making you a better person or worse? It's really that simple.

Is This a "Phase Cancellation," or Do You Just *Bug* Me?

We now know that in order for us to create the life we dream of, we must take complete responsibility for our reactions and become the masters of our emotions. The trouble, however, is that most of us can't get past our own natural reactive response when someone hits one of our triggers. In hindsight, we realize that we should have thought before we spoke (or waited to send that angry e-mail), but most often our instinctive reactions override our logical ones—*the rabbit, lion, or deer!*

The truth is that I struggled with my own triggers for years. It wasn't until I did the work that I finally realized it was always a certain kind of person who set me off; I just couldn't understand why or how to stop myself from reacting. Here I was a "healer" of sorts, and yet, when I came up against a certain personality, I'd start reacting from a place of ego—instinctive, scared behavior.

I want you to think about someone who upsets you the most. What is it about his or her personality that triggers you? Maybe it's a certain type of person who can always hit your hot spots and create an emotional charge in you. Spend a few minutes thinking about this, and then write down the qualities that bother you so much.

❖ ❖ ❖

Okay, we both know you aren't going to get along with everyone in the world—even other empowered people. It's impossible! The Law of Resonance states: When two energies are within close enough proximity to one another, their intrinsic energies come together causing either a "phase summation" or "phase cancellation." In simpler terms, this means that when you and someone else—with whom you've developed a significantly close bond—are together, any qualities that are similar will be amplified (strengths *and* weaknesses).

My friend Niko Sofianos, a spiritual fitness guru and sound engineer, compares the Law of Resonance and our relationships to composing and mixing sound tracks:

> Every instrument has a color—the technical term in music is "timbre." Therefore, when composing or "layering" sounds into a mix, the composer/mixer must know the "color" of each instrument so that he or she can create a harmonious or symbiotic sound experience. It's amazing how certain instruments, all beautiful on their own, can either complement or mask each other in a mix. Believe it or not, we all have the same mechanism inherently embedded into us. We all have a color, too, and we either "jive" with someone else (phase summation) or they end up "killing our vibe" (phase cancellation).
>
> I want you to picture the Law of Resonance like this: When you hit a note on the piano, you're not just hearing that one note . . . you're hearing it along with the resonance of the strings that influence or resonate with that note. Just as a piano represents all of the frequencies in a symphony, so does your whole persona; life is about being the conductor of your music—mixing with the right instruments at the right time in order to compose and sing your beautiful song. Remember, the Universe will correspond to the nature of your song—the mix of the frequencies you interact with most!

Knowing this information, ask yourself: *Is it a "phase cancellation" I'm experiencing with the individual who triggers me, or does this person really just bug me?* Maybe the reason you don't quite get along with your boss, sister, or father-in-law isn't a phase cancellation—perhaps you just aren't on the same wavelength . . . and nothing is going to change that right now. But wouldn't it be nice to reduce the amount of time you get "triggered" in a day, week, or month? Wouldn't it be a relief to make peace with the people in your life—those whom you can't eliminate so easily?

The only way to make peace in your relationships is by looking within and facing yourself. Here's something that might surprise you: I bet that if you look back at your list of unacceptable words from the exercise you did in Chapter 2, you'd notice that they're the same qualities you despise the most in others!

For me, my "nun" within still tries to shame me whenever she thinks I'm acting spoiled, mean, fake, or manipulative. And it was the spoiled, mean, fake, or manipulative people who triggered me the most!

Okay . . . what's going on?! Well, here's the truth. . . .

When certain people can evoke extreme emotions within you, you must realize it's never about them. They may have been thoughtless or cruel, but your defensive reaction is because they've triggered a "neuro-association" to a past pain—a quality that your ego has repeatedly told you is unacceptable; *a quality you secretly fear that you have possessed at times!*

I love the way Iyanla Vanzant explains this in her bestseller *In the Meantime:*

> Sooner or later, we must all accept that fact that in a relationship, the only person you are dealing with is yourself. Your partner does nothing more than reveal your stuff to you. Your fear! Your anger! Your pattern! Your craziness! As long as you insist on pointing the finger out there, at them, you will continue to miss out on the divine opportunity to clear your stuff. Here is a meantime tip—we love in others what we love in ourselves. We despise in others what we cannot see in ourselves.

The people who challenge you the most are the ones who confront you with the parts of your own personality that you still won't own or accept—the parts you were taught were unacceptable or negative, or the parts (believe it or not) that you can't see in yourself. *Yikes!* And when you see those same qualities in someone else, you reject them . . . and most often you reject the person, too.

What I love is how I've learned to recognize when my own ego is in action. Sometimes I catch it a little too late, but when I do see it early enough, I immediately elevate my emotions to a higher place so that I can see my "challenger" through a different lens. Do you know how many of my friends or associates were once people who bugged me the most? *If only they knew! What a laugh we'd have!*

It's amazing that when you change the way you look at others, the people you look at change. Those specific individuals may have triggered a negative reaction in me, but when I got past myself—my own ego—I found they were some of the most intelligent, funny, wonderful, empowered people I know. Not all . . . but some of them!

The more you make peace with yourself (and love all aspects of yourself), the less frequently you'll be triggered by others in your life. You'll learn to live and let live. Not everyone has to be your best friend, but you certainly don't need to get so worked up about things. (Remember, it's not real unless you choose to make it real!)

Know When to Call It Quits!

As you become more empowered—as your light becomes brighter—you'll find that hanging out with certain people who aren't where you're "at" will become more draining because they're draining your light (most likely, unconsciously). You have something they don't, and they want it. You can learn how to protect your light and not dim yourself to make others feel better when they're around you, but all too often, many people hold on to old friendships or relationships even though they know they aren't healthy or beneficial. You may have simply been in a friendship with someone for so long that it seems cruel to disassociate your-self from the person. Or perhaps an old friend or flame pushes hard to maintain a close relationship, even though it's becoming more of a struggle for you.

The fact remains, however, that the people with whom you surround yourself have the biggest external influence on your future than any other factor. It's no different for adults than it is for teenagers! Peer pressure can easily rob you of your success. You have to make sure that you're flocking with people who enhance your life force.

Try this exercise from my book *Simply . . . Woman!* and name the five people who are closest to you. Get out your R_x for Success and answer these questions about them: Are they successful, kind, and loving? Do they truly look out for your best interest? Are they content and happy in their own lives? Do they have a positive influence on you? How are they reacting to your desire to improve your life? Are they manipulative for their own gains? Are they controlling or totally accepting of you and your choices, whatever they might be?

In my own life, I did an inventory of everyone I knew and meditated on each and every person, asking myself, *Does this person add to my life force or drain me?* Then I asked myself a second question: *Whom do I need in my life to feel absolutely unstoppable?* I discovered that there were still a few missing links (for example, at that time I still needed a smart lawyer and a better assistant).

Once you're clear about what you need, go to Section 7 of your R_x for Success—your action plan—and write down these new discoveries!

With that in mind, you need to have the courage to take action in your life and be in charge of how, with whom, and where you spend your energy. It doesn't mean that you need to tell old friends that you're at a higher, more evolved place now. It just means that you need to start saying no more often, keeping yourself focused on the things that really light you up. Those who are your true-blues will understand and still be there in the long run. Sometimes you need to take small breaks to realize how much you miss some-one . . . or conversely, to see that it was time to move on.

Lovebirds and Bubble Baths

Sounds like the title of a catchy song, *doesn't it?* Actually, this is how my kids refer to me and my husband, Aaron—*lovebirds and bubble baths!*

We've created a home that exudes love: dimmer switches on most of the lights, candles lit almost every evening, soft music playing around the clock, and of course, bubble baths every night. My husband and I have made it a priority to show our children what love looks like on a daily basis.

Creating a home that resonates at the highest frequency is really quite easy. Simply think of lovebirds and how they would live. Did you know that they can't be apart?

The number one thing we stress in our home is *being together.* We do our very best to eat together, hang out together, clean the house together, go for dinner together, take daily walks together, drive the kids to their different activities together . . . and yes, even enjoy bubble baths together (well, my husband and I!).

Aaron and I talk about everything and anything—and we try to use our time cooking together as a means to keep our family close. We're all in the kitchen at dinnertime, preparing food, sharing our day's events, venting, laughing, crying, and sometimes even yelling. *Hey, we're a family!*

What I stress most to the kids is that it's okay to be upset, but you never, *ever* run away from the other person or think it's "the end." Nothing is ever as bad as it seems! As a family, we talk things out until we're done . . . and then, we move on and let bygones be bygones.

Let Go and Let God

There's nothing harder, in my opinion, than letting go of a relationship—especially one where you love the person so much but know that the relationship is no longer good for you. (This can even apply to a relationship you have with your work.)

Everyone has been there: you feel you've done all that you can possibly do and have given every last ounce of your being trying to make it work . . . and finally, "something" in you knows that you must surrender it. You must let go and let God.

Surrendering isn't weak; it isn't passive. True surrendering only happens once you've moved through your desires and taken action. You've been *so* willing to do whatever it takes to resolve things—to make them better—and finally, you realize that there's nothing left to do. There's nothing you can do. This is the moment when you shift into the highest realm of consciousness, letting go and trusting that whatever happens is the right thing.

You surrender to "what is" and let go of your desire to control things. You release the urge to make things the way you wish they'd be and accept that as long as you continue to honor yourself, all will work out perfectly. You surrender your need to be right, to be the best, and to prove yourself to anyone. You surrender your attachment to outcome and leave it in the hands of destiny. You allow God's plan for your life to unfold.

❖ ❖ ❖

Are you at the point in your life where you know that you must surrender certain things or people? Are you ready to let them go? Are you ready to set yourself free—*set them free?*

Perhaps it's your own story that you need to surrender. It may be an argument that you've held on to for far too long or a person that you once loved. Are you ready to let it go . . . *to let them go?*

If not, you must realize that you won't be able to sustain success as long as you're chained to the burdens of the past. Things change, people change, and *you* must change. It's a natural part of life. As long as you're stuck "back there," you can never be "up here," building a new, happy, prosperous future!

If you're ready to let go and let God, I suggest that you write a letter to whom you need to let go of. You don't even need to send your letter—in fact, I don't think you should. Letting go isn't about others letting go of you; it's about you releasing your *attachment* to them. Energetically, you can become so exhausted over time, simply because you've been "carrying" around so many people (and their stories and painful memories) in your mind, heart, and body.

One of the best exercises I've ever done (or have instructed my clients to do) for letting go is a "burning ritual." I want you to write a letter to whomever it is that you're still emotionally connected to. You may not have seen this person for 20 years; it doesn't matter.

It may be a letter to a parent (or both), a sibling, a friend, or an ex. You may realize that you have many letters to write! But in order for you to have all your emotional energy back, you must let this burden go. *You may think that just thinking about doing this exercise is enough. It's not! You must write and burn your letter(s) to experience the power of it.*

Write down everything you need to say, including how the person's actions have affected you and what it has cost you. Write about all of your self-limiting beliefs: when you've played it small or taken the easy way out, plus all the masks you created as you were trying to prove your worth.

This letter is not for anyone else but you, nor is it intended to hurt others. *It is to help you.* It may seem too hard or scary, but pour all your feelings out. It's time to clean it all up! You can't move forward when you're stuck in the past.

When you've finished the letter, send it to someone you trust. *Your letter must be shared.* If you don't have anyone you feel you can send it to, post it on the "Message Forum" at **www.crystalandrus .com** under an anonymous name. My coaches and I will read it.

After you've shared it, cried with it, claimed it, and understood how it has affected you, *burn it. You must burn it for the energetic ties to be released. This is the most powerful ritual you can do!* If you don't have a wooden fireplace or wood-burning stove, use your barbecue or even easier, just get a large tin lasagna pan. Lay your letter down, light it on fire, and watch it burn.

As you watch your words go up in flames, say good-bye to the person, pain, stories, and blame; say good-bye to the old beliefs. Why would you want to hold on to them any longer? Why would you want to keep replaying it? It doesn't serve you anymore. It's self-defeating and old. It's done, so move on! *If it was meant to be, it would be.* If this person was meant to be "the one," he or she would be. Let it go. It's time to get to the good stuff!

Eliminate Negativity by Loving Yourself

The easiest way to have an incredible relationship and find your soul mate is to develop an incredible relationship with yourself! Treat yourself the way you want to be treated. Take care of yourself the way you want your partner to take care of him- or herself. Do romantic things for yourself. Honor your needs, and speak to yourself with love and dignity. Be compassionate. Tend to your body and spend time pleasuring it—the way you'd want a lover to! Laugh at yourself, and don't take life so seriously. Let the small things go, be interesting, develop your passions, try new things, splurge on the odd treat, and nurture yourself with lots of TLC.

Start creating rituals for yourself. Make a list of things that you wish your knight in shining armor would do for you, and then start doing those things for yourself right now. Tell yourself every day that you're beautiful. Buy yourself fresh flowers for your bathroom, office, and kitchen. Run yourself hot bubble baths and surround your tub with candles. Play soft, soothing music and cook yourself fabulous dinners. Use your best china! Put on amazing outfits that make you feel great, even if you're not going out. Honor your body with massages, facials, or pedicures. Nourish yourself with foods that will love you back. *Respect yourself!*

PART II

Sustain

❖ ❖ ❖ ❖ ❖ ❖ ❖ ❖ ❖

realize that their emotions created that reality—not the other way around!

Empowered people, on the other hand, remain calm when there's a "situation" and put others at ease with their demeanor as well. They initially assume the best scenario and work forward. Their troubleshooting starts by examining the simplest explanation, then logically moving through their own mental checklist, minimizing the potential trouble. They see even the most stressful challenges through empowered lenses. They do immediate damage control and affirm that the past is the past (even the immediate past), so there's no point in dwelling on it. Empowered people assess the circumstances and instantly begin weighing their options, focused on finding a solution. They don't allow regret, shame, blame, guilt, or fear to overtake their mind-sets. Complaining is pointless. They keep their team/family intact (if there are others involved), knowing that if they can't figure it out, someone, somewhere, can. They continually refocus their minds should a negative thought try to enter. They understand that the moment of absolute certainty may never arrive, so they make their decisions swiftly and confidently, knowing that *almost* anything can be reversed if necessary. Once a decision is made, they move on because wasting their energy second-guessing themselves is just that: *a waste—pointless!*

Then they assume that everything will work out; they continue as if it were working. Should another solution be needed, they address it then, and only then. Their energy—mentally, emotionally, and physically—is too sacred to squander on anything unnecessary. They stay focused on what they want to happen and resolve to find a way to make that happen. Once the situation has been rectified, they quickly look at the part they may have played in causing the problem and adjust their plan accordingly—even if that means making a difficult decision. If it's in the best interest of the collective, they speak up— fire, hire, or reprimand those responsible—with dignity and respect. On the other hand, sometimes they let the mistake go if it's not worth berating a "normally good" employee or child.

If they're personally liable, they admit responsibility immediately, resolve it, and move on. They don't complain about it, rehash it, or give it another thought. They do *not* gossip!

Disempowered people are often so afraid of making the wrong choice, they make none at all. Not aware that you can "argue" for both sides of almost any situation, sometimes you must simply make the best choice possible. Doing nothing *is* doing something, and that something *is disempowering you!*

Is It a Solution or a Band-Aid?

Staying focused on solutions can be challenging from time to time; no one ever said that living an empowered life is always easy. How do you stay focused, for example, when your marriage is falling apart or when your teenage children are reckless and out of control? What if you've just been diagnosed with a life-threatening illness? How do you maintain your resolve when the recession is severely affecting your business and you're losing assets?

Here are five points to keep in mind when coming up with solutions:

1. Solutions should bring you closer to long-term relief. They're meant to raise you to a higher place.

2. There isn't always a perfect solution for every problem, but you must follow your gut and do what feels right.

3. The solution may not always be what you think you want or need. Be willing to surrender your notion of what success means in order to allow the unknown to unfold.

4. Solutions never forsake your dignity, respect, needs, or values. You may think being a martyr or

savior is commendable, but solutions that harm or devalue you (in any way) are *not* the answer. You can't help someone at the sake of hurting yourself.

5. Solutions alleviate pain, while bandages just stop the bleeding for a while.

Here's an example of how you have to take the high road when it comes to any difficult situation. The following is a case of a failing marriage:

"My Marriage Is Falling Apart! How Do I Stay Solution Oriented?"

When it comes to relationships, the first thing to remind yourself of is that you can't control or change someone else. With that said, matters of the heart are probably the most difficult challenges because they involve other people who have their own opinions, wants, and needs; and who will make their own choices, regardless of what you may want or believe they should do.

If you're in the crux of a failing marriage or relationship, you need to ask yourself: *What do I truly want?* Think about it. Do you *really* want to save the relationship? Do you *really* want this person to be your partner for life? If *not* . . . if you realize that you don't want to be there, you should spare your mate and make the courageous decision to tell the truth. I would never want someone to be with me who didn't truly want me. *Would you?* Have you convinced yourself that by staying you're sparing your partner's feelings? Let me assure you that the only feelings you're sparing are your own fear and guilt. Guilt-driven choices will inevitably spoil the outcome! Plus, remember that "whatever you fear you draw near." Either way, you're much better off being honest. Everyone deserves that!

If you do want to save the relationship and make it wonderful, you need to get very clear on *what you want* and *why you want* this union to work. You need to muster up all the fuel it takes to stay in a place of courage, willingness, and acceptance. List all the wonderful qualities your partner possesses and the ways in which he or she adds to your life force. Neither anger nor self-righteousness will serve you. Crying, blaming, whining, bitching, or "guilting" the other person to stay or change also won't serve you. Don't give the problem(s) anymore power! Stop talking about them and focus on solutions.

Once you're very clear on what you want and why you want it, ask yourself: *What would courage have me do?* The kind of courage I'm talking about would tell you to love and honor yourself, and trust that you'll only make choices that build your character and strengthen the sanctity of your relationship. It wouldn't tell you to save your partner or try to fix those around you. Just like no one is coming to save you . . . you can't save your mate either. Besides, who knows if it's really your mate who needs the rescuing!

Refocus your energy on yourself (*not* on bitterness or jealousy) by loving yourself, treating yourself well, exercising, eating healthfully, going out with friends who increase your life force, taking up activities that light you up, and getting yourself financially independent. Stop focusing on others! Then when you're with your spouse, you'll resonate at a higher level. You'll see your lover through different lenses, and one of three things will happen:

1. Your spouse will love the person you're becoming and want to join you in your new outlook. Inspired by your gentleness and understanding, he or she will begin to change and will soon shine more brightly, too. Your marriage will soar.

2. Your spouse won't change, and you'll realize that although you can't change a person, your newfound self-love prevents you from focusing on

his or her "flaws." You will live and let live. Your marriage won't be the center of your life—*you will be*—but it will be a wonderful part.

3. Your spouse won't change, and you'll have risen to such an empowered, beautiful place that you're able to lovingly set yourself and your spouse free. You know that you're both entitled to be happy and to be with someone who loves you unconditionally.

❖ ❖ ❖

When I separated from a man who (at the time) I believed was the love of my life, it was the hardest decision I'd ever made . . . yet deep down I knew I wasn't honoring myself in the relationship. The lies and betrayals had begun to eat away at my soul. Nonetheless, the day I asked him to leave, I also knew that I loved him more than I ever had. We didn't split out of a lack of love; we lacked trust and respect. It was my dear friend Debbie Ford who asked me straight out: "I know you love him, but do you respect him?"

I hesitated and began to make excuses for his behaviors, but she asked again: "Do you respect him?"

I sadly replied no, and we both knew I was done.

I realized that I had to completely and utterly surrender the relationship. If we were meant to be, he and I would be together, just not then. For the first time in my life, I put my spirit, my soul, before all else and took care of myself.

Every day for nearly a year, I would ask myself: *What would courage have me do?* And I would always hear my higher self say the same thing: *Do not call him. He hasn't done any of the work he needs to do for you to consider getting back together. Nothing has changed!*

I gave myself plenty of breathing time and grieving time. Did I cry? Every day for more than a year—and then some! For the longest time I wondered if I really loved him. Remember that *you can't know true love until you truly love yourself.*

I may have ached for him, craved him, and desired him . . . but it wasn't until I *surrendered* him—completely let go of what I wanted *him* to be, what I wanted *us* to be, what I wanted *me* to be—that I began to know what true love meant. At that moment, I realized that *it was what it was.* We had so much that was good together, but the tipping point had been shattered. I couldn't put enough back on my side of the scale to restore balance. Trust and respect outweigh any amount of chemistry and compatibility.

I knew I couldn't stay in a place of grieving—wishing and wondering and hoping—any longer. I'd been in this "city" long enough. I started by writing a good-bye letter to my once-supposed soul mate and burned it. I then made a wish list of all the qualities I needed in a man—traits that I'd never live without again and discovered were crucial to *my* spirit. (I was able to create my list of values only after doing the top-ten words exercise I gave you in Chapter 3.) Here's the list (taken directly from my journal) that I wrote that night while sitting at the bonfire:

The man I choose to spend my life with will be:

- *Affectionate*
- *Artistic or creative*
- *Passionate*
- *Sexy*
- *Financially independent*
- *Spiritual*
- *Confident*
- *Gentle*
- *Thoughtful*
- *Trustworthy*
- *Trusting*
- *Compassionate*
- *Powerful yet humble*
- *Insightful*

- *Innovative (a visionary!)*
- *Attractive*
- *Healthy*
- *Open and considerate (willing to give and receive!)*
- *Physically fit*
- *Patient (and not easily angered)*
- *Strong*
- *Soft*
- *Self-respecting*
- *Sweet*
- *Open-minded*
- *Understanding*
- *Generous (a humanitarian)*
- *Kindhearted*
- *Mature but fun*
- *Silly but dignified*
- *Secure*
- *Safe*
- *Loving (must love children, nature, and animals!)*
- *Clean (and a great smile and nice smelling!)*
- *Stylish (dresses well!)*
- *Sexual (a good lover!)*
- *Faithful*
- *Intelligent*
- *Enlightened*
- *Courageous*
- *Responsible*
- *Law-abiding*
- *Ambitious (but not excessively so)*
- *Balanced*
- *Devoted (Into me!)*
- *And did I say faithful!*

I trust this man will arrive, and I won't settle for anything less!

Four months later, in a whirlwind romance, I was engaged. It was the most "outrageous," yet most authentic, decision I'd ever made. I committed myself to a man who seemed to magically appear out of nowhere—yes, I'd found *my* prince. Some would say it happened because I had become a princess. Not the kind who wears a tiara or owns great lands, but the kind who knows the wealth within her soul . . . and is no longer afraid to share it.

Not surprisingly, it wasn't until I'd committed myself to someone else that "he" (my former mate of seven years) came back, professing his undying love for me. It was a test, my moment of reckoning. I chose my new fiancé. Years later, I look back now at that profoundly significant relationship—at the pain *and* pleasure—and realize that it was only because I truly loved him that I was able to leave. Had I stayed, I would have disabled my old love by preventing him from becoming the man he needed to be. And by doing so, I would have also disabled myself. We had outgrown each other, and he just didn't know it. *I did.*

As I mentioned, I also knew that a lack of love had nothing to do with why we had split up. What seemed like a huge failure turned out to be my greatest life lesson: *Love is not limited to boundaries, licenses, zip codes, surnames, or even this lifetime. Love is a place within. It transcends time . . . and asks for nothing in return.*

I made a decision to honor my life and respect my needs and dignity. I'm now with a man who holds me in the highest regard—from the biggest stuff, down to the tiniest details. Love shouldn't hurt, nor should it demean or drain you. It can be difficult, but all things are at times . . . so is a cranky two-year-old, but you'd never turn your back on her! The difference is, like the song says, *love lifts you up where you belong!*

Am I suggesting that you leave your relationship, as I did? *No!* But I do ask you to refer to the five points that outline solutions before you make any big decision.

Defusing a Difficult Situation

1. Take a deep breath and calm yourself down.

2. Never respond when you're upset—that may mean waiting 30 seconds or 30 hours! If you're not sure you're feeling calm, that's a good indication you're not! Don't respond, even if it means you need to take two or three days. Take time to calm yourself down first. This is crucial if you want to sustain success. No one wants to be involved with a loose cannon!

3. Nothing arrives unless it's time. Realize that you can find opportunities in all situations.

4. Negative, disempowered feelings will only hurt you.

5. If you make a mistake, admit it.

Success Doesn't Mean It Always Goes Your Way

Even the most empowered people wish things would *always* go their way, but they realize that without challenges, they'd never grow. It's only through discontent, unhappiness, frustration, desire, or pain that we are forced to evolve. Everything arrives with divine timing.

We may not understand why something has happened, and we may even interpret certain events as terrible dilemmas because we can't see the bigger picture. But wouldn't it be far more empowering if we were to consider that all is as it's meant to be and that everything will work out perfectly, as long as we honor ourselves and treat others with dignity and respect? From that perspective, we would intuitively know that we *will* find the needle in the haystack—as difficult or impossible as it may seem in the moment—if we really need that needle!

Disempowered people, on the other hand, focus on the problem rather than potential solutions. They think if they talk about it *a lot*—sharing their misery with anyone who will listen—it will somehow alleviate the pain. These kinds of people lose friends fairly quickly (or only have a few to begin with) because most of them are tired of hearing their constant complaining.

I always remind myself that *those who complain are in pain!* Talking about it excessively doesn't deal with it . . . focusing on solutions does! *Yes,* you do need to discuss problems, but then you must find a way to accept them or fix them.

Disempowered people will look for the worst and dwell on the negative. They recite their "story" as often as it seems appropriate to the conversation (they also try to find opportunities to make the conversation fit their story), explaining only their side and pointing out reasons why it's not their fault in order to justify their lack of success. They may even think they're normally "positive"—survivors who simply share their tales of woe to keep you from falling prey to their challenges.

❖ ❖ ❖

Let me give you an example of Karen, a client of mine who was struggling with her weight. Every day she would wake and sneak to the bathroom to step on the scale. If she was down a pound, it was a good day; if she was up a pound, it was a bad day. When she walked by mirrors, she was disgusted by her reflection, inwardly shaming herself and beating herself up, but also resolved that "one day" she would make peace with this obsession and finally lose weight and feel good about herself. During the day, Karen would peruse the Internet to find out if any new weight-loss secret had been revealed or to search for articles about celebrity diets and how the rich and famous stayed thin.

Each evening, after a long, exhausting, *unfulfilling* day, she'd complain about her body, complain about her weight, and complain about the "reasons" why; then she'd step back on the scale "just to see." Usually heavier than in the morning (due to food and water retention throughout the day), Karen would head to bed even more depressed and would rest her hand on her stomach while lying down just to remind herself of what she desperately wanted: *a flat belly!* As she drifted to sleep, frustrated and depressed, she'd vow to get back on her diet *tomorrow!*

Karen would start off great each morning, but by dinner she could no longer overcome her cravings. She blamed her husband for not eating healthy and exercising, and felt that her lack of success was because he wasn't supportive enough. She was just so fed up with her body, energy level, and growing health concerns; and with each day, she felt worse and worse. Losing the extra weight had become almost impossible, even while being relentlessly focused on the problem! *How did this happen to her?*

Remember that staying focused on what you want—on *solutions*—regardless of the situation is imperative. In Dr. Wayne Dyer's book *The Power of Intention,* he explains what he calls "the face of expansion," the power of spirit to help you expand your awareness of what's possible in your life. He stresses that whatever you think about expands. So if you focus on the problem, it will grow in intensity, size, and seriousness. It will become very real to you! He encourages you to instead be "open to the 'knowings' that you have always had inside you that have quietly been guiding you."

After sharing her story and discussing other aspects of her life with me, Karen was open to trying my approach. She knew she had to take the focus off her weight and how awful she felt about herself. I hoped that I convinced her that *beating herself up was never going to lift her up!*

She began by writing her new mantra on recipe cards and placing them around her home:

In order to do better, be better, and look better,
I must *first* feel better about myself!
What can I do right now to make myself
feel a little better?

First things first, she needed to throw out her scale and set her purest intentions to the Universe. She closed her eyes and imagined exactly how she wanted to look and feel, then described it in full detail in her journal.

Karen focused intently on becoming confident, happy, energized, sexy, fun, fresh, outgoing, fit, strong, bold, powerful, inspired, inspiring, authentic, motivated, healthy, and beautiful. Just saying those positive words made her excited, even though a small part of her kept trying to pull her back to her old ways of feeling and behaving. Karen wanted to feel excited and alive again! She understood that her "trickster" was just fighting for its life, not realizing there was a more empowered way of doing things and that she was worth more than the life she'd been living.

She also realized why she couldn't lose weight. She was *so* bored—with herself, her life, her body, her sexuality, her relationship, her job, her cooking, her house, and her family. Even the idea of taking a trip didn't excite her like it did when she was a teenager on spring break! She began to think about how she used to feel years ago—when she'd fantasize about the amazing life she'd one day live . . . and back to the time when losing weight was effortless.

Karen needed to focus on things that would add to her life, lift her spirits, and make her feel more vibrant. Losing weight, she was learning, wasn't about losing out on things! It was about gaining what she really needed—the things that fed her spirit! Deprivation and self-loathing couldn't possibly create empowerment. By solely focusing on her body, food, calories, and fat percentages, she'd been avoiding the truth.

I asked her why she would avoid making herself feel good, and *fear* was the response I got: *fear of being magnificent.* Marianne Williamson explains this concept the best in her blockbuster book *A Return to Love:*

> Our deepest fear is not that we are inadequate. Our deepest fear is that we are powerful beyond measure. It is our light, not our darkness, that most frightens us. We ask ourselves, Who am I to be brilliant, gorgeous, talented, and

fabulous? Actually, who are you *not* to be? You are a child of God. Your playing small doesn't serve the world. There's nothing enlightened about shrinking so that people won't feel insecure around you. . . . We were born to make manifest the glory of God that is within us. It's not just in some of us; it's in everyone. And as we let our own light shine, we unconsciously give other people permission to do the same. As we're liberated from our own fear, our presence automatically liberates others.

Feeling good about yourself also comes from having the integrity to honor your truest needs. Karen investigated different options for exercising and made a weekly plan for her meals and grocery shopping list. She enrolled in a cooking class to learn how to make healthy, decadent meals. She knew she had to make herself and her needs a priority. No more ordering pizza or buying hot dogs just because the kids wanted them! And no more letting them play video games all evening, while she sat on the couch sipping wine, either. Besides, she acknowledged that she was setting her own children up for a lifetime of poor eating habits, unhealthy cooking, and little activity.

Now when Karen wakes up, she asks herself how she feels on a scale from one to ten. No matter what number intuitively comes to mind, she thinks of just one thing she can do in the next five minutes that will make her feel a little better . . . something to move her from, say, a three to a four or a six to a seven. Throughout the day (for at least 21 days), Karen's assignment was to stay aware of her "level of joy" and find just one more thing—one soul-driven thing—to lift her spirits higher (and these have nothing to do with counting calories!).

I asked Karen to make a list of rituals (we talked about this at the end of Chapter 6) that she can look at anytime her level of joy is diminishing. *Beating yourself up never lifts you up!* Here are some of my ideas: say a kind word to yourself, stand up taller, hold your stomach in and chest out, do your top-ten value words (if you haven't yet), drink a glass of water with lemon in a beautiful goblet, take your dog for a walk, take your neighbor's dog for a walk, enjoy a hot bubble bath with candles, put on lip gloss and mascara, recite your favorite mantra five times out loud, get a pedicure, whiten your teeth, play with the kids, play with your husband!, smile at everyone you pass, play a game of golf (or learn to play golf), lift weights, listen to fun music, listen to fun music while you lift weights, enjoy a hot cup of coffee or green tea, sing out loud (*really loud*), smell the roses, plant some roses, go for a walk in the sunshine during lunchtime, clean your house, pay someone to clean your house, clean someone's house who could really use the help, call an old friend, call a new friend, make a friend, take a cooking class, cook a delicious and healthy dinner, eat dinner using your favorite china, bring a delicious dinner to someone who could use it, enjoy an exhilarating yoga class, learn to teach yoga, read a great book (or an erotic one!), read to someone, take a long bike ride, pick up the phone and call that "one" person you've been avoiding, meditate, join a baseball team, watch the sunset, paint the sunset, take dance lessons, get a massage, buy a great new scarf, sit at the water's edge and write, send someone a postcard (from where you live), take photographs, start a scrapbook, jog outside, listen to the birds sing, make love, take a drive with all the windows down (even better in a convertible), pray, learn to play a musical instrument, get a facial, relax in the sun (with sunscreen!), paint your bedroom, pet your cat, get a cat, kiss someone you love, hug and kiss your loved one again, create a fantastic playlist on your iPod or MP3 player, do something outrageous, do something peaceful, go on a first date (even better—go on a first date again with your spouse), wear lingerie (no matter what your size), have an orgasm, have another orgasm, have fun, get out of the house, spend more time in bed . . . the list is endless!

Esther and Jerry Hicks explain this idea so beautifully in *The Astonishing Power of Emotions:*

> If you were as sure of *who-you-are* as the inner part of you is, you also could turn your undivided attention toward the new ideas; and if you were to do that, you would feel an eagerness for life, a clarity of mind, and a vitality of body that would be indescribably wonderful. . . . Now this is the most

important part of this story of creation and of your physical, human, Leading Edge creative part in it: *In the moment that a new-and-improved version of life is born out of the life you are living, you have the option of aligning with the new idea or of resisting it.*

In every situation, choose to focus on what you want to feel rather than what you currently feel, and visualize what you want rather than what has happened in the past . . . and act accordingly. Do not *ever* entertain the option that it might not work out! If you've got a back door, you'll use it!

Remember that when you focus forward rather than back, your spirit expands into a creative force that only seeks solutions. Success will be yours, every time!

What If It *Doesn't* Go Your Way?

Does success mean that everything *always* turns out the way we want it to? *No!* In fact, when most of us look back on our lives, some events that seemed to be a failure in the moment were exactly what needed to happen to change the direction of things. They make us stretch and grow! They help us become stronger and better able to overcome smaller problems. We must remember this one simple statement: *Nothing is ever as bad as it seems.*

In his book *Tough Times Never Last, but Tough People Do!* Dr. Robert Schuller reminds us that "the problems you face in your life will not be forever. Only those who persist and those who tough it out will stand in the end and succeed in their life." Setbacks are a part of everyone's success. If you aren't willing to fail, then you aren't willing to succeed!

You can always hold your head high if you know that you've done everything you could possibly do. Then, and only then, you must surrender your attachment to outcome, knowing that what may seem like a defeat is simply a new opportunity for growth. This is the time to take a breather. Stop working "it."

Release it, accept what is, and fly back to your perch like the wise owl. Let go and let God. Take a hot shower and get some sleep. Go out and have some fun—and when you feel like you have your wits and humor about you again, reassess the situation through new lenses.

Sometimes it's in the quiet moments of nothingness that the answer comes. When we're always doing—thinking, wondering, pondering, worrying, attacking challenges head-on—we miss out on the simple signs . . . the whispers of our spirit trying to show us the easier way.

Be Proactive, Not Reactive!

Proactive people create their lives rather than reacting to outside stimuli. Conversely, reactive people are affected by *everything:* their feelings, circumstances, conditions, and environment. They complain a lot and always have an excuse. They might be funny or sarcastic, but over time they become a drain—one bad thing after another happens to them! Proactive people, on the other hand, take action, seek solutions, and are driven by their *values.*

Here are some of the examples of *reactive* language:

◆ "That's just the way I am!"
◆ "They won't allow that. . . ."
◆ "I have to do what?!"
◆ "I don't have enough!"
◆ "I can't!"
◆ "If only . . ."
◆ "It's not my fault!"

Here are some examples of *proactive* language:

◆ "Let's look at our options!"
◆ "Let's do our best to make it happen!"
◆ "No worries!"

Chapter Eight

UNCOVER ANY FLAWS IN YOUR PLAN

"Our greatest glory is not in never falling,
but in rising every time we fall."

— *Confucius*

Is there a problem with your plan? How can you know? Perhaps you haven't given it enough time. If you've done the proper due diligence, just allow the seeds of creation to germinate and the roots of success to grow.

If, however, your gut—or your result—tells you that things aren't moving in the right direction, you need to uncover any flaws in your plan as soon as possible. This takes courage, as most people would, sadly, rather be right than empowered. Admitting to flaws in your plan might mean that you've made a mistake . . . it might mean accepting temporary defeat in order to regain ground, becoming brutally honest about yourself and your choices, good and bad. It might mean having to totally reinvent yourself, change plans, and rewrite the future! But you might be so stuck on what "I want" that you aren't willing to see the signs or trust in *what is.*

You need to continually check in with your "Success Tracker" (in your R_x for Success binder) and be honest with yourself. Are you hitting your targets? If not, reassess your plan.

Five Ways to Ruin Your Success!

1. *Ask for more than you're willing to give.* Others catch on quickly and soon resent your selfishness.

2. *Give more than you're willing to lose.* Eventually, your well will run dry, and you'll become an "angry giver," poisoning your success with your own resentment and bitterness.

3. *Ride other people's coattails.* Once they take off their coat, you're screwed!

4. *Be unwilling to bend in the wind.* Things change, people change, and plans change; you must change if you want to carry on successfully. Rigid rules and rigid thinking will inevitably ruin your success. Reinvent yourself—or your plan—if necessary!

5. *Procrastinate or slow down just as things are getting going.* Believing that momentum will carry you is *not* the way to sustain success. Momentum without forward motion won't last forever!

Did You Do Your Due Diligence?

As quoted in an article in Wikipedia, *due diligence* is defined as:

> . . . a term used for a number of concepts involving either the
> performance of an investigation of a business or person, or
> the performance of an act with a certain standard of care. It
> can be a legal obligation, but the term will more commonly
> apply to voluntary investigations. A common example of due
> diligence in various industries is the process through which
> a potential acquirer evaluates a target company or its assets
> for acquisition.

Whether you're considering seriously dating someone or getting married, starting a business, investing your money or time,
buying a home, choosing a real-estate agent or financial advisor,
partnering with someone on a project, hiring an employee, rent-
ing your home, or finding a contractor (the list is endless!), you
must always do your due diligence. If you don't, you're entering
an agreement blindly. It's not an insult to protect yourself or
your loved ones. In fact, it's crucial to make educated decisions
as well as going with your gut! Take the time now, if you didn't
do so before you made a big decision, to learn as much as you
can about the person or project (or situation).

So . . . *What Now?!*

Okay . . . so you didn't investigate everything as thoroughly
as you could have, or something completely unavoidable and
unforeseen has cropped up and things aren't working out
completely as planned. *No worries!* If you're totally invested—
emotionally, financially, and/or spiritually—you simply need
to *uncover the flaws* in your original plan and correct them.

Uncovering a flaw may be as simple as owning up to the
truth that you haven't budgeted properly or spent accordingly. It may mean you've lied or manipulated, procrastinated,

avoided a step, or let an important decision slide. You've forgotten, overlooked, or haphazardly missed something.

Don't let the problem drag on. Find it and fix it! Do it differently (always with integrity), and then let your mistake(s) go. Write a new story, a fresh plan! Few things in life are irreversible. Victimizing yourself or beating yourself up isn't noble or humble. It's self-defeating and self-punishing, as well as being pointless and a waste of time. Remember that it's impossible to align your thoughts, words, and actions with success if you're stuck in shame or embarrassment. You can't achieve your goals if you feel awful . . . it's really that simple! Learn your lesson, and let yourself off the hook.

Uncovering the flaws in your plan, just like staying focused on solutions, isn't always fun or easy. It sometimes means swallowing your pride, which takes an enormous amount of accountability, determination, and willingness. Know that it takes courage to admit that things aren't quite right, and the worst thing to do in this situation is to deny that things are off track. That doesn't, won't, and can't work toward sustaining your success.

Maybe uncovering the flaw in your plan might even mean that you'd have to admit you've *enjoyed* using your story to let yourself off the hook—in other words, you've been trying to make others responsible for your life. Sometimes people stay stuck because they're punishing themselves, somehow believing that if they condemn themselves, they'll be absolved in the next life. *Not true!* God forgives everyone!

(*Note:* The truth is that God doesn't feel sad or mad, especially regarding you! He loves so much "bigger" than any one of us can conceive. He understands all—your reasons, fear, pain, regret, temptation, avoidance . . . *everything*. It isn't God who is mad at you. *You are mad at yourself.*)

Perhaps the reason why you can't uncover the flaw is because you don't really have a plan! You've been flying by the seat of your pants, and it has finally caught up to you. Do you understand the importance of having a plan now? *Without a plan, you plan to fail!* If this is you, you must go back to Chapter 3 and get to work! Figure this out now or you'll stay stuck in life.

The Unstoppable Force of Momentum

According to the dictionary, momentum is "the strength or force gained by motion," and it can help predict how successful you will be and how quickly you will achieve your goals. You know the momentum is flowing when you're on a roll and progressing quickly.

The equation for momentum is mass multiplied by velocity. Anything (including you) that's in motion has momentum, all moving at various speeds, depending on its mass. The size of your desire is the "mass," while the "velocity" is how much action you take. In other words:

Burning Desire x Persistent Action = Massive Momentum

In the early stages of creating, it's extremely important to uncover any flaws in your plan that might slow you down. The temporary failures or initial setbacks can really stall things, but once the momentum builds, very little can get in your way. And as your momentum increases, it will become easier to blow through challenges with ease and power. Here are three key steps to creating and sustaining momentum:

1. **Take immediate action!** In order to build momentum, you have to start moving. Once you start, it will be easier and easier to maintain your progress and sustain success. Take action today!

2. **Take massive action!** Slow and steady may win the race between the tortoise and the hare, but when you're running with other hares, you better start fast and never slow down. Whatever you need to do to achieve your goals, start building powerful momentum by

doing *massive* amounts of action—in other words, even when you win a few small races, keep heading to your ultimate finish line!

3. **Stay in the action!** Many people begin to slow down or take a break when they start noticing positive results. *Huge mistake! You're killing your momentum!* If you've just experienced some success, whether it was a great presentation or an awesome dinner date, use that energy and confidence you've gained and continue moving. Your reward is the high you feel! *Isn't it incredible?!* Wouldn't you love to remain in this elevated state? This is empowered living!

Uncover the Lies

If you've ever been to one of my Simply . . . Woman! Retreats, you'll know that participants do a "truth exercise," where I explain how powerful your own life can become once you find the courage to uncover any lies (including traps, denial, fear, desire, wants, and needs) and speak the truth. When your life feels hard—whether it's regarding business, relationships, or health—it's because somewhere you aren't living your truth. *You aren't aligned with who you really are.* You've actually begun to believe your lies, "your story." You, consciously or unconsciously, use your story and may even "work it" to justify your situation.

How do I know if I'm still stuck in my story? Well, if you're still sharing your story, for whatever reason, you're still stuck in it!

You may not even realize that you're in a story or a "life trap" because you're so committed to it that it defines you. At one time in your life, this "tale of woe" (maybe that of the tough girl who could never count on anyone, or the sweet girl who cares too much about others at the sake of herself) has worked for you. And the reason why you've been able to sustain the old story—the one of unfulfilled dreams and numerous letdowns and failures—is because you created it. Remember, if you didn't create it, you can't sustain it!

It goes back to the steps on creation: if you're sabotaging yourself, it's because somewhere *you are out of integrity with who you really are.* You may be living what someone else has convinced you of or still trying to prove your parents wrong (or right) . . . but it isn't the truth for you. You may actually believe the reasons you tell everyone else as to why things aren't working out. Remember, you created your reality and not the other way around!

Are you ready to face *your story* once and for all and be done with it? Where in your life are you still lying or obscuring the facts? What are you still too embarrassed to admit to? What are you covering up? What must you stop or start? What are you unsuccessfully trying to fix on your own? Where are you still trapped?

Uncovering the lies is easy once you truly see the story you've been telling (and living) for so long! Only you can be honest with yourself and decide to make things right, let the old story go, and reinvent a new and more empowered version. The truth, no matter how hard it may seem in the moment, will always set you free! And admitting it just may surprise you. Even the biggest mistakes lose their power—and you'll be able to forgive yourself—when you set them free. Remember, *you must feel successful before success will manifest in your outer world!*

In order to release your old story (which might actually be the flaw in your plan—that is, you're stuck in your past), you must ask yourself what you have been more committed to. Your pride? Anger? Fear? Blame? Guilt? Shame? Have you been more committed to making excuses than taking action, to being right than getting help, or to hiding your mistakes rather than assuming accountability and moving on? Shame will keep you stuck. (As I share in my book *Transcendent Beauty,* to truly move on in life, you must *name it, claim, grieve it, and release it!*)

Every Failure Brings You One Step Closer to Success

How many times can you get back up after you've been continuously knocked down? How many times will you go back and uncover the flaws in your plan? The right answer is: *As many times as it takes for you to figure out what you're doing wrong and correct it!*

That's all you can do . . . and you know what? People respect you when they see you coming back, trying to get it right. *That's staying power!*

What do Jim Carrey, Halle Berry, Kelly Clarkson, Ella Fitzgerald, Martin Sheen, Charlie Chaplin, Chris Gardner, Cary Grant, Kelsey Grammer, Daniel Craig, Djimon Hounsou, Harland "Colonel" Sanders, David Letterman, Hilary Swank, John Woo, and John Drew Barrymore have in common, besides the fact that they're all extremely talented people? They were all homeless at times while trying to build their career! People may have looked at them as failures. Perhaps at times they wondered themselves why they were so intent on achieving their dreams, but in the end, temporary failure was what brought them great success.

Failure is such an awful word—its implications are so negative sounding. I believe that failure is experience: *specialized knowledge.* I feel like I could give any writer the most brilliant advice needed to become an internationally best-selling author, but it's not from my successes. It's from my failures! I learned firsthand what I did wrong, as well as what I did right. It was my shortcomings that stoked the coals of desire, becoming my fuel to prove myself *to myself* (and to a few naysayers).

In the beginning, I truly thought I had one shot—a single opportunity that could make or break my entire career, and every time I walked onto a stage, I left it wondering if I completely blew it. Many times I had some lucky breaks—with sold-out books and people waiting hours to meet me—but there were many times that I'd come home, cry, and kick myself for ruining a great opportunity. *Why didn't I do it differently?!* But I learned . . . and I'm still learning!

Eventually, even after my biggest messes, I'd pick myself up, dust myself off, do whatever damage control I needed to do, and then get right back at it. I'd try to uncover my flaws so that I would do better the next time! Every talk made me more confident, and every misstep ultimately made me stronger. Every success gave me just enough momentum to drive me to the next place. *This applies to everything in life! Be accountable, apologize if necessary, and get back on the horse.*

If you compare it to marriage, you don't consider your relationship over just because you have a disagreement—even if it's a huge one. You let the dust settle and talk it out. You kiss and, hopefully, make up. You learn from your mistakes and grow. You become better.

If part of your plan isn't working, rework it. If the new idea doesn't help, change it. Continue to find solutions until it does work! You may have to completely reinvent things, so you need to release your attachment to how it's going to happen and be willing to do it differently.

Remember that temporary defeat means only one thing: something is wrong with your plan. As Napoleon Hill states in *Think and Grow Rich:*

> The most intelligent person living cannot succeed in accumulating money—nor in any other undertaking—without plans that are practical and workable. Just keep this fact in mind, and remember when your plans fail that temporary defeat is not permanent failure. It may only mean that your plans have not been sound. Build other plans. Start all over again.

Chapter Nine

SWAY THEM YOUR WAY

*"You can make more friends in two months
by becoming interested in other people
than you can in two years by
trying to get people interested in you."*

— *Dale Carnegie*

How did things go *so* wrong when they were once *so* right? We often ask ourselves this when we've forgotten to consider the feelings of those around us. We nagged, bitched, complained, and accused, solely focused on the problem at hand. We pointed out other people's flaws and were quick to judge. We had all the "answers" . . . if only they would have listened. *Sound familiar?*

Throughout this book, I've asked you to ask yourself: *What do I want to feel?* Now it may shock you when I tell you that one of the best ways to get what you want is to help others get what they want.

Make It a Win-Win

My mother had a saying while I was growing up: "You can catch more bees with honey than with vinegar." In short, it means that if you want to win someone over, be sweet. You will never get your way or influence others by being bitter and sour.

Now I'm not suggesting that you should act fake or give false flattery, but when you sincerely focus on the good qualities in others, you bring out more of their good qualities! Remember, *where attention goes, energy flows . . . and it grows.* By appreciating others and considering what they want, you're able to create a winning combination. It simply doesn't work if just one person is happy . . . at least not in the long run. In time, children rebel, spouses leave or shut down emotionally, employees cost you money because of their bad attitude, co-workers complain, and your success runs out.

Criticizing others will never win anyone over or get someone to do something your way. In fact, most people dread condemnation and will do almost anything to avoid feeling small, inadequate, or unimportant. Child, husband, or daughter-in-law . . . they'll avoid your complaints and nagging at all costs even if it means a fight when they finally get home (*if they come home!*). No one wants to be around a know-it-all. No one wants to be micromanaged or constantly reprimanded.

The best way to bring out the best in others is to truly care about them—their feelings, needs, and wants—and help them achieve their own personal success while you're achieving yours. Do you know what motivates your children? Your employees? Your spouse? Your mother? Your boss? Here's a clue: you may think it's money, toys, or presents (they may be the initial incentive), but these things won't keep anyone motivated for long. People want to feel valued, wanted, needed, and appreciated! Everyone desires love and acceptance. Learn to *really* listen—and genuinely care about what you're hearing—and you'll soon discover that your needs will be met as well.

Active Listening

When you make a conscious effort to actively listen to people, your relationships develop on deeper and more intimate levels. Don't you feel respected and appreciated when someone genuinely listens to you? Doesn't it feel good to know that what you say is valued?

Everyone knows the Golden Rule: "Treat others the way you want to be treated." Active listening means that you *listen to others the way you want others to listen to you.* Here are some listening tips I culled from a great article written by Susie Michelle Cortright:

1. *Stop everything*—even if it's just for two minutes, and face the person who's speaking to you. You'll be amazed how much people appreciate your attentiveness, and they'll move on to their next activity far more easily than if they were fighting for your attention. Two minutes can feel like 20 for a child who's desperate to sing you a song or read you a story!

2. *Pay attention.* Never become preoccupied with your own thoughts when someone is speaking to you. If you have to, take brief notes in order to concentrate on what's being said. You can hear approximately four times faster than you can speak, which often means that most people tend to focus on the next thing before a speaker has the chance to complete his or her thought.

3. *Tune in and ask questions.* Cortright says to "respond appropriately to show that you understand." In other words, smile, nod, raise your eyebrows, and so on. Say things like "Wow," and "I see," and ask direct questions

such as "Then what happened?" Lean in toward the speaker and make eye contact. (Just don't overdo it so you become annoying!)

4. *Don't butt in.* If you're listening to someone criticize or complain about something you did or said, hear the person out and resist the urge to respond until it's your turn to speak. Cortright says: "The speaker will feel as though their point has been made. They won't feel the need to repeat it, and you'll know the whole argument before you respond."

5. *Sum up the main idea.* Cortright advises us to "ask questions for clarification, but, once again, wait until the speaker has finished. That way, you won't interrupt their train of thought. After you ask questions, para-phrase their point to make sure you didn't misunder-stand. Start with: 'So you're saying. . . .'"

I Don't Care What You Want!

One of the biggest mistakes when trying to win others over, whether in business or pleasure, is telling them *what you want* without considering *what they want*. For example, how many times have you written the "objective" on your résumé as something like this: "I am passionate about helping others, and I want to work in a great environment. I am a team player"? *Well, good for you, but who cares what _you_ want.* (At least that's what the boss thinks!)

As a business owner, *I* want to hire someone who's objective looks more like this: "I am passionate about your products and eager to work with your dynamic team. I want to help increase your revenue and find new ways to expand your brand. I want to help get your message out to the world." *Wow! Who would you rather hire?*

If you want to be hired or sell your services or product, figure out what your company or clients need and find a way to fix their problems or build on their solutions. Just as John F. Kennedy said in 1961 at his inaugural address: "Ask not what your country can do for you—ask what you can do for your country." Using his approach, why not ask what you can do for your family, spouse, company, and so on—*not* what they can do for you? With this new way of looking at things, you may initially think that you're denying your own needs, but I assure you that you aren't! Once you've found out what motivates your team, client, boss, employee, spouse, mother-in-law, or children, you'll know how to encourage, influence, and bring out the best in them—making yourself indispensable.

It's no different than falling in love: if you go out on a first date and expect him to give you everything you want—to cater to your every whim and wish—you'll never meet Mister Right, even if he were right in front of you. If you're too focused on your wants, he'll instantly be turned off and you won't have the chance to get to know the real him.

Instead, go out with a big smile and great outlook, and notice the best in everyone you meet—find out what others want and need. You may be shocked by what you discover . . . and in turn, you'll instigate a desire within others (including, perhaps, Mister Right) to please you, too! Remember this: *Sometimes when we step outside of ourselves, we recognize we are in the presence of (undiscovered) greatness.*

This is similar to the story Dale Carnegie shares in his book *How to Win Friends & Influence People* about Florenz Ziegfeld, the most dazzling Broadway producer, who had a reputation for finding diamonds in the rough:

> Time after time, he took drab little creatures that no one ever looked at twice and transformed them on the stage into glamorous visions of mystery and seduction. Knowing the value of appreciation and confidence, he made women feel beautiful by the sheer power of his gallantry and consideration. He was

practical: he raised the salary of chorus girls from thirty dollars a week to as high as one hundred and seventy-five. And he was also chivalrous; on opening night at the Follies, he sent telegrams to the stars in the cast, and he deluged every chorus girl in the show with American Beauty roses.

I Love You Just the Way You Are

The best movie to watch when you're single or going through a breakup is *Bridget Jones's Diary* (at least it was for me). Bridget Jones is a thirty-something, single, working woman living in London. The movie itself is a modern-day *Pride and Prejudice,* and the main focus is on Bridget's love life. Over the course of the movie, she becomes involved in two romantic relationships: the first is with her charming and handsome boss, Daniel Cleaver; and the other is with the stuffy human-rights barrister Mark Darcy. Without sharing whom she ends up with, I will tell you why she falls so madly in love: *She found love and acceptance exactly as she is—and is not expected to change and conform to please her mate.*

Isn't that what most of us want: to be loved and accepted just the way we are? And yet how can that ever happen when we don't even like ourselves "just the way we are"?!

Instead, what so many people try to do (especially when they're attempting to sustain success) is to change others and make them be who they want them to be. Maybe you've done this, too. You *really* think you're helping others by pointing out their faults, calling them on their mistakes, and showing them how to do things the "right" way. Parents often do this with their children (especially teenagers). It's also common to act this way with a spouse, in-laws, and employees; and some people even do this with their boss, thinking they're showing off how wonderful and smart they are. *Big mistake!*

The number one way to sabotage your success—whether in your marriage, with your kids, at work, or in running a Fortune 500 company—is to disregard others and make them feel wrong, unappreciated, or unworthy.

When I was only 17, I was promoted to assistant manager of the retail store where I worked. I went to high school full-time but still managed to work a 40-hour workweek. I never turned down a shift. When I went in to work, I always put on my best face and best smile, and I outsold all the other employees. They never resented me, or at least they never acted as though they did. They'd often stand back and watch me in action, then ask what my secret was. Back then, I couldn't quite explain how I was able to sell so well. I never felt manipulative or that I was selling someone something they didn't want. After listening to a customer, I'd race around the store and bring her the perfect shirt, pants, or coolest pair of shoes. I'd point out her best features and show her how to accent them. I'd be attentive and genuinely interested, forgetting about my own aching feet or growling stomach. My clients walked out feeling fabulous, and in turn, I felt pretty good myself! The shift would end, and I'd be shocked how fast the time flew and how much money I'd made. I had fun! Besides, the staff was paid on commission so that made selling even more exciting!

My manager was just as successful in his own way. He had the entire staff wrapped around his finger without ever being inappropriate or sexual. We all adored him and worked our butts off for him. When he promoted me, he told me his secret: "Never *ever* be afraid that someone you've hired will outshine you. A good manager hires good people then creates greatness in them. When your store can run itself because you've empowered your employees, you are a great leader." His advice stuck with me, and by the time I was 21, I was successfully running my own company. Sure, I was a hard worker who smiled all the time, never brought my problems to work, and never asked an employee to do something I wasn't willing to do myself . . . but I believe my success came because I made my clients feel important and my staff feel even more important.

We all need to feel appreciated, valued, and significant. That is one of the biggest reasons to sustain success! Sadly, some managers or bosses think that giving positive reinforcement is a sign of weakness in a leader. Many parents think that hovering over their kids, demanding respect (but not showing any), and inflicting emotional pain through criticism, sarcasm, or indifference is the way to keep teens on the straight and narrow. From what I've learned about teenagers, though, negative gets negative! Harping will just make them rebel all the more.

Most people already realize when they've screwed up—they don't need you to point it out. They know if they got lost driving, arrived late, or failed a test; and they really don't need you to hound them or make them feel worse than they already do. The best way to help others make a change or recognize that they're screwing up is to first check in with yourself to be certain your advice is warranted and absolutely necessary. Useless criticism is shaming, often ambiguous, and can come off as a personal attack.

If you must criticize someone constructively, first ask yourself if *you* selected the right person from the get-go. If you didn't do your due diligence, how can you expect your employee, friend, or partner to become someone he or she isn't? You get upset—frustrated by his or her incompetency—but aren't you really just upset with yourself because you tried to bandage a situation rather than find a proper solution (*the right person for the job in the first place*)?

We do this all the time, especially in our love relationships: We meet a potential Mr. Right who has baggage we don't think we can deal with but convince ourselves that we can change him. And when that doesn't happen, we become angry and bitter. Useful or constructive criticism, on the other hand, may initially take him aback but will ultimately leave him with some answers and solutions. He'll feel like you care about him. Useful criticism can be helpful—in *small* doses—to instill greatness in someone!

If you feel compelled to criticize someone, be sure you focus first on his or her good qualities. Once the person trusts that you're doing this because you genuinely care, respectfully explain what's wrong, minimizing the problem rather than dramatizing it.

Lavish Praise—It Goes a Long Way!

Every so often corrections must be made and you may have to discipline someone, but lavishing praise goes much further in shaping your company, relationships, and/or children. It's not that criticism doesn't work at modifying behavior, but over time, continual disapproval—always pointing out flaws—creates resentment, animosity, and anger in the recipient. Sure, you may have set your children on the path to greatness with your constant harping and stern rules, but they'll hate you by the time they achieve their goals. They may attribute some of their success to your endless pushing, but the personal and psychological damage you've done won't be worth an ounce of their achievements.

On the other hand, when you single out specific personality traits and accomplishments that are desirable, you raise your kids' self-esteem. They'll be initially motivated to please you in order to receive more encouragement, but eventually, they'll be compelled to live up to the grand reputation you helped create for them.

I mentioned earlier during my struggle for success that every talk made me better and every failure made me stronger. Every success provided me with just enough fuel to drive me to the next place. Failure toughened me up (*that's for sure!*), but it was the successes, as small as some were, that gave me the momentum to keep going.

Studies have shown that positive reinforcement—praising even the slightest improvements—is more effective than criticizing mistakes or even ignoring them. Dr. Elizabeth Hurlock, a world-renowned psychologist and author of many books, including *Child Growth and Development,* demonstrated the effects of praise on children in a study. Dr. Hurlock divided fourth and fifth grade students into three groups. The first group consisted of students who were identified by name and praised in front of other students for their good performance. Students in the second group were also identified by name in front of other students but were criticized for their poor performance. Finally, students in the third group were completely ignored, although they were in the classroom to hear the other students being praised or criticized.

The results showed that after the first day, the students in the groups that were praised or criticized performed better than the ignored students. *Did you read that?* The kids who were ignored did *worse* than the ones who were criticized!

(*Note:* And we wonder why our marriages fail, our children rebel, our employee productivity is down, and/or our pets won't obey us?! We simply can't create anything if we aren't putting in the time. The grass isn't greener on the other side—it's greener wherever we water it!)

By day two, the criticized students showed a significant decline in their test scores, while the praised students continued to excel. By the fifth day—only five days in—the criticized group was performing equally with the ignored group. Think about it: the only thing that had changed for these young kids was the way they were spoken to (or not spoken to). No group contained a majority of smarter kids or troubled kids, but the messages they heard reinforced their outcomes.

You perform better when you feel valued, important, and worthy enough! You know this by now though, don't you?

You must feel successful in order to be successful!
You must feel good in order to do good.

Adults are no different than children. We all want to be acknowledged, praised, and respected. We all want to feel special. We want others to believe in us—to trust and have faith in our ability. We need to believe in ourselves!

For that matter, animals are no different than humans. Treat all living things with love, encouragement, and sincere appreciation, and you'll have won over the world. Trying to demand that people respect you—even a bratty stepchild or defiant teenager—will never win them over. As Gandhi said so beautifully: "Be the change you want to see in the world."

And if you must correct someone, remember that the *way* you do so is as important as *why* you are doing it. Always begin with praise followed with your suggestions for improvement. Always use dignity and compassion. Besides, it's a small world . . . you never know who could end up being your boss one day!

Chapter Ten

TRUST IN THE PROCESS

"I know God will not give me anything I can't handle.
I just wish He didn't trust me so much."

— *Mother Teresa*

In April 2007, Michael Vick, the former star quarterback for the Atlanta Falcons, was arrested for running a dog-fighting ring out of his Bad Newz Kennel in rural Virginia. The 47 pit bulls removed from his property lived terrible lives, including being chained in dark, dank basements and given electric shocks if they didn't perform well in fights. The best fighters earned the best treatment, but some, like "Little Red," had their teeth removed so they could be used as "bait dogs" to spar with the champions without hurting them. Vick admitted to personally hanging and drowning dogs that wouldn't fight.

One would wonder if any of these vicious dogs could *really* be rehabilitated. To many, euthanasia seemed like the only option.

Vick, who pleaded guilty, was sentenced to 23 months in prison and ordered to pay close to a million dollars for the lifelong care of the dogs that could be saved. Here was a man who was adored by thousands of cheering fans. He had a career and reputation that could have sustained him for a lifetime, if he had been smart, played by the rules, and lived with integrity. Instead, he allowed himself to become a victimizer—a light destroyer!

I tell this story not to upset you, but because its outcome is a testament to the power of love and trust.

Just over half of the dogs were adopted or placed in foster homes, but 22 were deemed so dangerous that they were sent to an animal sanctuary in Utah called Dogtown. For the first month, the trainers spent continuous one-on-one time with the dogs, even sleeping with them at night—in the same bed. There was no "breaking" the dogs' spirits, no yelling, hitting, punishing, or taking things away . . . just loving each and every dog, continually reaffirming the message: *Trust us . . . we aren't all the same! We won't ever hurt you!*

Within a year, all of the dogs were transformed into beautiful, loving creatures! Leo, a tan, muscular pit bull, visits cancer patients as a certified therapy dog in California. Hector, who bears deep scars on his chest and legs, is about to start training for national flying-disc competitions in Minnesota. There are no bad dogs, only bad masters!

Trust Is the Seat of the Soul

What does Michael Vick's story have to do with sustaining success? *Well, let me explain. . . .*

When my troubled 15-year-old brother, Edson, first came to live with me, everyone, including his own parents (my father), warned me that I was in for more than I'd gambled. Drugs, drinking, fighting, expulsion from school, a joyride in a stolen car, parole officers, lie after lie . . . I had my work cut out for me! My dad had just had a small stroke and was about to put my brother in a 90-day drug rehabilitation center because he was too weak and unable to cope with his son's behavior. Since my dad was resigning, I decided to step in.

Day after day, I reminded myself about those 22 dogs who were once deemed unfit and unlovable but who soon became man's best friend. As my brother was unpacking and settling into his new room, my father wanted to fill me in on his son's latest screwups, wanting to prepare me for the worst. I told my dad I didn't want to know anymore. I knew enough already— *I'd done my due diligence!* I knew I was probably in over my head a bit, but I wanted my brother to have a fresh start—a clean slate—an opportunity to rewrite *his* story. I knew Edson had no understandings of how to create success and of the need to clean things up in order to reinvent himself. I realized that I would have to have *a lot* of patience and compassion. Who knew how long it would take for him to straighten up? But I also knew he wouldn't have arrived unless I was ready—*and he was!*

For the first three weeks, I let my young brother sleep, *a lot*. I cooked good meals and kept the house super clean and super quiet, except for our round-the-clock soft music. I ran him bubble baths, lit candles, and burned incense. I spent time with him and spoke to him as if he were already on the mend. I prayed a lot, too.

I got him started with guitar lessons and listened for hours as he practiced. My husband thought I was babying him, my siblings thought I was insane, and my children were a little jealous. But something inside me knew that my young brother had simply lost trust: in his parents, in his family, and in himself. Using drugs was just his way of self-medicating, and the trouble he'd been getting into was a cry for help. (Like dogs, people will do almost anything to get attention!)

I knew that all he needed was a loving "alpha wolf." He needed to be part of a pack and know that he would be provided for. He needed to know that he mattered and was loved.

Four months later, after many tough days and long nights, he had his breakthrough—the dam broke and the tears began to flow. Five hours later, he emerged, literally looking like a new person; it was like a butterfly who had just broken free of its cocoon. Fifteen years of pain, fear, anger, disappointment, and sorrow poured out of him that evening with me. His eyes, for the first time in years, were so clear; his face so fresh; his smile so innocent . . . he was ready to love and be loved. He reminded me of how he was as a toddler. Edson apologized for all the pain he'd caused everyone and told me that he never realized how much we all loved him (our dad included).

There have been many times (before and after that night) that I've felt like throwing in the towel—real transformations don't happen like they do on a 30-minute TV sitcom. My brother isn't out of the woods yet, but he's definitely headed in the right direction. I have faith. And whether or not he figures it all out now or later or never, I know that I've loved him as much as humanly possible. I know that *he* knows he's deeply loved.

Through this experience, I realized that time is the greatest gift we can give another person—our attention, validation, conversation, hugs, listening, and talking . . . just simply being together. There are moments when I feel like I'm giving more than I can afford to lose (or more than my family can lose) and I have to pull back. As hard as that is and as much as I don't want to, I know that I can't help anyone at the sake of myself or my family.

As far as my brother's situation, time will tell. I love him regardless of the outcome and only know for certain that the journey is his own. The real question is whether he'll learn to love himself. I think he's beginning to. . . .

❖ ❖ ❖

Regardless of what it is you're trying to create, you must keep the faith. *Trust is the seat of the soul.* Things don't always happen when you think they should or how you expect they will, and even when times seem darkest, you need to have faith that love will conquer all. As Julia Cameron writes in *The*

Artist's Way: "There is a path for each of us. When we are on our right path, we have a surefootedness. We know the right action—although not necessarily what is just around the bend. By trusting, we learn to trust."

Every day ask yourself, *What would love do?* And with that in mind, your truest answers will always come through and guide you.

Build Your Trust Muscle

What do you say to a mother who lost her child in a tragic accident or to a husband who lost his wife and the mother of his baby to cancer? What do you say to individuals whose family members were murdered, their homeland ripped apart . . . destroyed by war? How do you tell these people that they need to trust in the process?

Asking someone who has experienced the pain of death to allow the seeds of creation to germinate isn't exactly appropriate or fair. How can you really tell someone who's grieving and in deep pain (and perhaps feeling very angry) to resonate at a place of love and acceptance? No matter who you are or how enlightened you may be, it takes time to process certain situations, and there's no set date when you'll be ready to see things through different lenses.

A remarkable story—one that I implore you to read—is Immaculée Ilibagiza's. I had the pleasure of dining with her a few times, and her light glowed all around her as if she were an angel. Then and there, I knew that Immaculée was a world-class light worker.

In 1994, her world was ripped apart when her native country of Rwanda descended into bloody genocide. Her entire family, except one brother who was out of the country, was brutally murdered. Miraculously, Immaculée survived the mass slaughter. For 91 days, she and seven other women huddled together silently in a tiny bathroom while hundreds of machete-wielding killers hunted them.

To learn more about her story, including the moment she actually faces the man who brutally murdered her family and *hunted* her, you must read her powerful book *Left to Tell.* Here's a brief passage that shows that despite the heartbreaking sorrow she endures as a survivor, she's also able to trust and have faith in life and God.

> I knew that my family was at peace, but that didn't ease the pain of missing them. And I couldn't shake the crippling sorrow that seized my heart whenever I envisioned how they'd been killed. Every night I prayed to be released from my private agony, from the nightmares that haunted my sleep and troubled my days.

She goes on to explain how God had answered her prayers in a beautiful dream:.

> From that night onward, my tears began to dry and my pain eased. I never agonized over the fate of my family. I accepted that I would always mourn and miss them, but I'd never spend another moment worrying about the misery they'd endured. By sending me that dream, God had shown me that my family was in a place beyond suffering.

❖ ❖ ❖

Trust, just like a muscle, can be built—even after it's been almost totally destroyed. No one can explain why bad things happen to good people or why others are so dark . . . so evil. I'm sure Immaculée would say that evil people are the victims of victims, destined to live in torment and regret. I believe that it's in the times of our greatest challenges and sorrows that we come to know the real meaning of life—the fragility of mortality, the sacredness of love, the beauty of passion, the power of desire, and the tenderness of God.

I'll never forget the night that he (what I assumed to be God) spoke to me through my writing, which I shared earlier in this book in the Preface:

> *Can you imagine my children thinking I've forsaken them? That I won't give them what they desire and dream of? That I won't help them?*
>
> *If only they would realize that I've given them the greatest gift of all: free will, free choice, and the ability to take action; as well as my unconditional love, support, guidance, and encouragement!*

The hand of fate will touch us all. Faith, like trust, isn't an insurance policy against pain or suffering. It's a knowingness that although we can't always understand the *whys*, we surrender our questioning, believing that love will see us through. We know the strength of the human spirit.

Remember that it's not what happens to you, but what you do with what happens that shapes the future. *Your life matters!*

Chapter Eleven

Ask for help

"Ask and it shall be given you;
seek and ye shall find;
knock and it shall be opened unto you."

— *Matthew 7:7*

Like many people who are trying to sustain success, I never wanted anyone to see me sweat. And as much as I do believe that you don't want your new boss, investor, or spouse to think that you can't do something—that you're having second thoughts or that you're giving up before you've even gotten started—it's crucial to have a sounding board. You must have a support system.

I know there are times in certain situations that you simply can't allow yourself to show defeat, concern, or fear, but pretending that you never have any problems will inevitably exhaust you. Trying to do it all *will* defeat you. Asking for help isn't weak; in fact, it's smart and makes you stronger.

Share the Struggle

As an author who facilitates healing retreats and courses, I used to feel like I couldn't show anyone that I had problems—that it would be like a marriage counselor who gets divorced or the child psychologist who has a terrible relationship with her own child. *Wrong assumptions on my part!*

I thought I had to be perfect and have all the answers, all the time. Although I encouraged other successful women to attend my retreats or enroll in my empowering programs, I could never seek help for myself. Even when I mentioned that I might hire a personal trainer, some of the people in my life blurted comments like: "If you can't motivate yourself, what hope do the rest of us have?!" or "I thought you taught this stuff, yet you're going to get help? That's ridiculous!"

I know now that my outer world was merely projecting back to me what I believed. At the time, I believed that asking for help *was* ridiculous. I was smart enough! I shouldn't need help from anyone else, let alone a personal trainer. *What was wrong with me?!*

I refused marital counseling when my first marriage was on the rocks. *How could someone help me sort out the affairs of my own heart?* When I'd messed up my finances, I was embarrassed; there was no way I was going to admit my mistakes or failures to anyone. *I'd sort it out on my own.* And when I was in the depths of despair after my breakup, I thought antidepressants were for "other people," not for someone who was as strong as I was. When my doctor suggested that I might be up against something bigger than me, I was speechless. *He had no idea who I was or what I was capable of achieving!*

I never thought that other people who sought help were weak; I just didn't know how or who to ask to help me. No one in my family had ever gotten help—for anything. They were the "masters of all trades" . . . or so they thought. My parents believed that they could fix anything by themselves, but after their marriage self-destructed, they both slowly fell apart—physically, financially, emotionally, and spiritually. How could that happen to two such incredibly talented, beautiful, smart, successful people? The answer: *pride!*

No one in my family ever considered that they may not have all the answers, and we were taught to keep our "dirty little secrets" to ourselves. No one needed to know our business. My family doesn't even talk about their sicknesses—I found out *a year after* my grandmother was diagnosed with lung cancer because she didn't want to worry anyone. It took a week or two to learn about my father's stroke. My parents couldn't or wouldn't show their weaknesses (especially to each other), but the great thing about life is that no matter what has happened, it's never too late to change. *It's never too late to face the music and clean things up!*

It Doesn't Mean You're Handing It Over!

Asking for help doesn't mean relinquishing accountability. Just because you hired a nutritionist, personal trainer, financial planner, housekeeper, interior decorator, therapist, naturopath, bookkeeper, personal assistant, and so forth, it doesn't mean that *they* are now responsible to fix your "stuff" and keep you all cleaned up. Hired help is exactly that—*help*, not a savior. You are still the captain of the ship! Your life is still in your hands. Never relinquish control over your destiny, and never blame others if things don't work out. You are in charge. Do your due diligence!

Get the Help You Need

As I've learned by the grace of God, you don't need to have all the answers. Henry Ford, one of the richest men in human history, said this to an interviewer who was asking him a ton of pointless questions: "Will you kindly tell me *why* I should clutter up my mind with general knowledge . . . when I have people around me who can supply any knowledge I require?" It doesn't make you stupid or weak to ask questions, share your struggles, and get the answers and help you need. Don't let an addiction, fear, embarrassment, shame, guilt, or uncertainty slow you down. Reach out to someone who's better off than you are— someone with a proven track record—and get yourself sorted out immediately, even though shame will try to convince you to do otherwise!

You must be willing to do what it takes and allow yourself to receive help! Don't be bothered by how others may or may not perceive you. You can't worry that you won't be loved, liked, or accepted. You must surrender your attachment to outcome and trust that when you ask, you will be given, when you seek, you will find, and when you knock, it shall be opened unto you.

Most of us ask, pray, and wish for miracles, but we don't allow good fortune to manifest in our lives because we aren't willing to receive it. We aren't willing to receive love, encouragement, guidance, or even compliments. *But allowing is really where all of our personal power lies.*

Maybe you aren't used to being helped. Are you afraid that if someone helps you, you'll be indebted to him or her . . . and you don't want to owe anybody anything? Maybe someone has helped you in the past and then hung it over your head, or perhaps you won't allow yourself to trust in others. Are you so afraid that if others discovered the real you, they'd judge you? Are you embarrassed to show your mistakes; afraid to reveal any weaknesses? Maybe you were taught it, too, like I was. But as I mentioned, I've learned firsthand that trying to be perfect is exhausting.

In the last chapter, I shared the story of the pit bulls that were rehabilitated with love. People are a lot like dogs—we're pack animals, too! We aren't meant to be lone wolves. For those who don't have loving families with whom they can share their struggles and successes, they must find support elsewhere. We live in a world where so many of us now work from home. We can return e-mails and schedule meetings in our pajamas, but

eventually we become isolated and lonely. We don't even realize we're depressed because of a lack of *real* human contact.
(And I don't consider "contact" to mean when the kids and
your husband get home from school and work.) For those of
us who are privileged enough to work from home (as I am), we
must get involved in other fun activities and find empowering
groups to join.

I also recommend that you seek counseling or coaching if
you're struggling at all—personally or professionally. You may
be an expert at what you do, but remember that two heads
are better than one! I connect with my dream-team coaches
at least once a week. If one of us has had a particularly tough
week, we share it, as well as brainstorm about ideas we may
have.

Please let down your walls, release your preconceived
notions about who you think you're supposed to be and what
you (or others) are supposed to do. Be willing to allow the
miraculous to unfold in your life. God only wants for you what
you want! Get the help you need so you can view the bigger
picture of *who you really are* and what you're capable of achieving. Don't let your ship sink and crew drown simply because
of pride.

Don't Forget about the Big Guy Upstairs!

I shared this story in *Transcendent Beauty,* but I think it's
powerful enough that it needs to be shared again:

About [five] years ago, I was in a hotel room about
2,500 miles from home, getting ready to give the biggest seminar I had ever given. I had been up since 5
A.M., meditating, doing yoga, and praying. I needed
every bit of power and strength I could acquire . . . and
yet I still felt so afraid and unsure.

This seminar, I thought, *could make or break my
career.* As the last hour ticked by before I was to leave

my room, I got down on my knees, lifted my arms to the sky, and looked up. I begged God not to let my words fail me as I walked onstage later that day.

In that moment, I experienced something that would forever change my life: I had a complete surrendering, wherein an overwhelming knowingness overtook my entire being. I'd prayed all my life, but this was different. I was suddenly filled with an exhilarating energy that, at the same time, gave me absolute calm and peace. I instantly knew that my words would never fail me, for they weren't *my* words. I began to overflow with tears and was completely overtaken by a euphoric feeling of bliss.

I walked out on that stage as a new woman. I was no longer trying—*I'd become.* And I knew it.

I realize now that it doesn't matter if you've only known this feeling for a day or for a thousand years, once you know it—you know it. . . .

For weeks afterward, everyone who entered my presence told me that I looked more beautiful than they'd ever seen me. I knew what it was from!

❖ ❖ ❖

Prayer is one of the most powerful ways to transcend beauty, protect your light, manifest miracles, and connect with the Divine Universal Collective Energy. Prayer must be of a positive intent, with the unwavering gratefulness and belief that your prayer has already been answered. When you pray with gratitude, in effect, you acknowledge that you trust implicitly that all will be as it's meant to be and that all will work out perfectly. As Neale Donald Walsch wrote in his thought-provoking book *Conversations with God:* "You will not have that for which you ask, nor can you have anything you want. This is because your very request is a statement of lack, and your saying you want a thing only works to produce that precise experience— wanting—in your reality."

For me, I have an almost never-ending dialogue with the Divine. I chat with him as I run, while I drive, or whenever I feel unsure or afraid. Simply knowing that God will never forsake me gives me an innate sense of power. Perhaps it's the knowingness that I'm a part of him and he's a part of me. This daily conversation is my constant reminder that I am never alone and that as long I "check in," all my needs will be answered.

In the wonderful little book *Your Needs Met,* Jack and Cornelia Addington have created spiritual mind treatments, "scientific prayers," that we can use and apply in our own lives. The very first prayer is one for attracting abundance, and its simple message captured me: "There is no lack but a lack of faith in God. . . . The will of God in me is Wealth, not want, but I must not hinder the will of God by belief in lack, or by telling God how my good shall come to me."

The undisputed power and protection of prayer can even be documented scientifically. In the most widely publicized study, cardiologist Randolph Byrd studied 393 patients who had been admitted to the coronary care unit (CCU) at San Francisco General Hospital. The study was to observe the therapeutic effects of praying to a Judeo-Christian God. To evaluate the effects of prayer in the CCU population, a prospective randomized double-blind protocol was followed. Over ten months, 393 patients admitted to the CCU were randomly placed into one of two groups: the prayer group (192 patients), where Christians outside of the hospital prayed for them; and the remaining patients were the control group, made up of 201 patients who weren't prayed for. Neither the patients nor the hospital staff knew which group they were in. The results, while surprisingly wonderful, didn't astound those who prayed. The consistent and overwhelming data suggested that prayer has a beneficial, therapeutic effect, as those being prayed for had far fewer instances of congestive heart failure, fewer cardiopulmonary arrests, and fewer cases of pneumonia. They also relied less on ventilator assistance and needed fewer antibiotics and diuretics.

One of the most astounding studies was a survey of 131 controlled experiments, where it was found that "prayed for" rye grass grew taller, prayed-for yeast resisted the toxic effects of cyanide, and prayed-for test-tube bacteria grew faster!

No matter what your religious beliefs may be, *I* pray that you embrace your God with appreciation and gratitude, knowing that your prayers will be answered. *Amen!*

Chapter Twelve

INVEST IN WHAT MATTERS

❖ ❖ ❖

"Creation is about <u>action.</u>
Sustaining is about <u>reaction.</u>"

— *Crystal Andrus*

*D*o you believe in preordained destiny, or do you believe that you have absolute control over your life? Here's something to consider. . . .

According to Sir Isaac Newton's third law of motion: "Whenever a particle *A* exerts a force on another particle *B*, *B* simultaneously exerts a force on *A* with the same magnitude in the opposite direction." His law is stated as: "To every action, there is an equal and opposite reaction." Here's an explanation of the law from an article by the Physics Classroom:

> A force is a push or a pull upon an object which results from its interaction with another object. . . . According to Newton, whenever objects A and B interact with each

other, they exert forces upon each other. . . . Consider the flying motion of birds. A bird flies by use of its wings. The wings of a bird push air downwards. Since forces result from mutual interactions, the air must also be pushing the bird upwards.

Other examples of this law would be:

◆ If you press a stone against your finger, your finger presses back on the stone.

◆ If you kiss your husband's lips, his lips are kissing yours back.

This law also applies to what I've been discussing. You can't engage in any behavior without the behavior engaging in *you*. If you engage in behaviors that build your character, strengthen your resolve, and make you feel like a good person, those behaviors will engage you also. In other words, you'll become a person with character, resolve, and integrity. Remember that where attention goes, energy flows, and *it* grows. Good or bad!

This law also suggests that if you dabble with darkness, darkness dabbles back at you. So if you touch evil, it will touch you back. Forces *always* come in pairs (pairs of equal and opposite action-reaction). To every action you take, there's an equal and opposite reaction (don't confuse the word *opposite* to mean negative, antagonistic, or in the reverse).

How do you react when you don't like what you get, what you see, or what happens to you? How do you react when you recognize an injustice? Do you respond from an empowered place—courageous, willing, faithful, and loving? Do you speak your truth with calmness, dignity, and respect? Do you realize that you will receive an equal and opposite reaction?

Your life is based on a culmination of all your actions and reactions—as well as the actions and reactions of the people around you (another reason to be careful of the people you

INVEST IN WHAT MATTERS

spend time with). Reconsider the question I posed at the beginning of this chapter: Do you believe in preordained destiny, or
do you believe that you have absolute control over your life? If
you believe in scientific laws, you must believe that you're in
control of your life based on Newton's third law of motion: for
every action there is an equal and opposite reaction. *But wait!*

If you believe that an all-powerful God decides your fate,
what about the statement from the Preface of this book: "If
only they would realize that I've given them the greatest gift
of all: free will, free choice, and the ability to take action. . . .
Creation is about *action* and sustaining is about *reaction.*"

I think, either way, <u>*you* *are the co-creator of your life!*</u>

The Law of Reciprocal Action

The best way to understand reciprocal action is to think
about this quote from the Bible: "Whatever a man sows, this
he will also reap," or the Chinese saying: "If a man plants melons, he will reap melons; if he sows beans, he will reap beans."
Reciprocal action simply means: *You get what you give.*

The "giving" part of reciprocity doesn't only apply to mate-
rial things—in fact, it even surpasses words and attitudes!
The thoughts you think send off a wave of energy that, like
a pebble dropped into a pond, ripple out in a circular motion
and touch everything in its path. The ripple from the pebble
continues toward the shore, and once it reaches the land it
begins to move back to the center of the pond . . . back to the
spot where the pebble was first dropped. You, like the pebble,
can't touch anything without causing a ripple effect. Your emotions are so much more powerful than you realize. Remember
how angry words and thoughts affected the water crystals in
Dr. Emoto's work? Your thoughts are like boomerangs, sending
out a frequency that will inevitably ricochet back to you, thus
explaining how and why *you get what you give.*

These laws reinforce why you must treat others the way in
which you would like to be treated! Do you now see the power

you hold? Your loving thoughts and actions can shift you toward complete empowerment. And as more and more people embrace this, the whole level of human consciousness will be elevated.

Be of Service

Hopefully knowing the third law of motion and the law of reciprocal action will motivate you to live your greatest life. What I've found is that the more I give, the more blessings are bestowed upon me. The gifts I receive aren't always monetary but, nonetheless, they are just as worthy!

I want to tell you a short story that reinforced to my husband and me the magnitude of the law of reciprocity. Keep in mind that I'm not trying to impress you with our deeds; I want to show you how this law works in so many often unseen ways.

A few weeks ago, my husband and I were driving in the rain. Sitting on the edge of a street corner, we caught sight of an old man desperately trying to smoke a wet cigarette butt he'd just picked up from the sidewalk. As we passed him, I instinctively said to my husband, "I feel so terrible for him. I wish we could give him some money."

"Money isn't really the answer. He needs a hot meal," my husband replied.

We drove up the road to a local restaurant to order some quick takeout. Spinning our vehicle around, we raced back, hoping the man hadn't left his spot. Thankfully, we spotted him just beginning to make his way up the road, and I called out to him. Soaking wet, dirty, and dragging a small shopping cart filled with odds and ends, he stumbled toward our car. He reeked of alcohol and looked very thin and frail, with missing teeth and a matted beard that hung nearly to his chest. He apologized for the state he was in and appeared to be embarrassed.

I asked him if he was hungry and would like a hot meal. He said he would. I then asked if he'd like my umbrella. He shook his head and replied that he loved the rain: "It was a cleansing from God."

Passing him the hot meatball sandwich and chocolate milk, we bade him well and continued on our way . . . only to realize the road we were on had come to a dead end. Turning the car around once again, we headed back to the spot where we'd just left him. What happened next left Aaron and me speechless. . . .

This homeless man had no idea we were coming back. He'd sat down and carefully opened his meal, placing it in front of him. We watched as he looked up to heaven and said a prayer before taking a single bite, finishing with the sign of the cross. He then looked down and noticed us watching, and flashed us a big grin and a thumbs-up.

It was truly an authentic moment. Here was a man who was starving, wet, dirty, and tired, yet he was still filled with gratitude and reverence. It was such a powerful experience for both of us because we were confronted with our own self-righteousness; we believed we were better, I guess, because our clothes were nice and clean. We had felt so noble handing him that meal, thinking we were so wonderful, only to realize how wonderful *he was*. Giving to him gave us back far more than I can explain in words.

That's the thing with experiences—until you yourself experience an act of pure, genuine gratitude, you can only *slightly* imagine what it feels like. Gratitude lifts you to the highest expression of yourself!

❖ ❖ ❖

There's nothing more important for long-term success than for us to remember to invest in what matters most: *the people we love and care for, along with those who need our love and care.* So many of us, unfortunately, invest countless hours on mindless activities. We waste our most precious commodity, filling our hearts, minds, bodies, and souls with garbage. Then we wonder why we feel rotten!

> **Do good and you'll feel good!**
> **When you feel good, you are good.**
> **When you are good, you attract good.**
> **It's that simple—you reap what you sow.**

We often hear great leaders tell us to serve others, and we sarcastically think: *I serve every day! I never seem to stop serving people—my spouse, the kids, my parents. . . .*

Being of service means doing something for someone *whom you aren't expected to take care of but want to anyway.* No matter how little you have, surrender your attachment to things. It's ironic: when you least need the money, it arrives. (Let me clarify *need*—it doesn't mean you have plenty of money and don't need anymore. It means that you've realized that happiness can't be bought.) When you aren't desperate for Prince Charming, he shows up. When you care more about things than people, you've lost the meaning of life—life will never feel authentic and "rich," no matter how much wealth you acquire.

A hot coffee for the crossing guard, an offer to babysit for that stressed-out new mother, a home-cooked meal for the lonely senior who lives down the road, or even a dollar placed in someone's cup . . . give something (big or small) every day, and I promise that your own cup will runneth over!

Chapter Thirteen

NEVER GIVE UP

*"Our greatest weakness lies in giving up.
The most certain way to succeed is always
to try just one more time."*

— *Thomas Edison*

I remember the night, years ago, when I sat down to watch *The English Patient.* I was alone, and it was getting late in the evening. I'd read the raving reviews and saw it win the "Best Movie of the Year" at the Academy Awards. I figured it would have the power and intrigue to keep me awake. I was really excited about it! However, 75 minutes into it, I could barely keep my eyes open and wasn't following the plot. *What was everyone talking about?! This movie was long and boring.*

Disappointed, I turned it off and went to bed. The next day, I noticed the cassette still in the VCR (yes, it was before the days of DVDs!) and for the sake of finishing it, I hit the play button. I really did want to see it and thought that maybe I was just too tired to enjoy it the night before. I'm so glad I did, because what unfolded for the next 75 minutes mesmerized me. All the seemingly scrambled pieces of the puzzle were coming together; and I was completely pulled into the drama, passion, and heartbreak.

Then I rewound the nearly three hour movie and watched it all over again, this time, hanging on to every word. I was spellbound! I rented it again the following weekend, and as I watched it, I sobbed as if it were the first time. Imagine if I'd never seen it through to the end! (As soon as I could, I bought the VHS tape and eventually the DVD version. And when the sound track came out, I bought that, too!)

My nearly missing out on watching *The English Patient* is such a simplistic but effective example of what quitting too soon can cost you. How many things have you missed out on because you gave up too soon, perhaps because you've been taught that immediate gratification outweighs long-term success?

We live in a world where the "waiting time" for all things has been cut in half, from long-grain rice to Internet speeds. We want what we want the minute we want it, and if we don't get it fast enough, we give up. Here's what I think: If we're willing to quit that easily, we never really wanted it in the first place. Right? *Easy come, easy go.*

Unless you focus on and pursue success with an unbending drive, you won't stay the course. Go back and read your R$_x$ for Success. Revisit your drivers, values, priorities, and commitments. It's normal to have the odd bad day—moments where you want to quit—but you simply can't give up if you expect to sustain success. It doesn't happen overnight.

I remember, not too long ago, when a friend of mine said that I was an overnight success. I reminded her of the years and years—*countless hours*—I'd put into my burning passion to write books that made a difference, to work on a TV show that had substance, to facilitate healing retreats, and to create passive streams of income. She laughed and recalled a time 15 years earlier when we were jogging, and I was telling her that I was going to be a published author one day. *Overnight success?!*

Try again! This has been 20 years in the making, and I'm still not where I want to be!

Do you think the greatest leaders and most influential people today didn't sometimes question their resolve and perhaps wonder, *Why am I doing this?* If you think for a minute that those who've achieved greatness haven't felt the hills and valleys—haven't felt like giving up—you're fooling yourself. It isn't because of luck or opportunity (these things may open a door), for long-term success is forged because of one magical ingredient: *staying power.*

When the Going Gets Tough, the Tough Get Going

Okay, so maybe that title is a cliché, but honestly, it's easy to stay motivated and focused when you're just getting started—when everything still feels exciting—whether it's your first year of business, first year of marriage, or first year of college. Those who sustain success know that once the fun is over, the real work—and eventually, payoff—begins. As I remember hearing a woman say on Geraldo Rivera's talk show many, many moons ago: "It's easy to be Rocky in bed for one night. What makes a real man is being like Rocky for a lifetime!"

It's no different than when you first join the gym, and you're highly motivated: every week you notice a new muscle hurting, a few more pounds gone, and your pants fitting more loosely. It's exciting to create, running on adrenaline and exhilaration! But how do you sustain that success, month after month, year after year? The answer is staying power, which some people call willpower. It's the only thing that will keep you going day after day.

Willpower can often be confused with being "inflexible," "tough," or "overly ambitious," but it's only those who carry on despite all odds who become successful beyond measure! What I've learned is that when failure is not an option, you'll find a way to make it work.

Where There's a Will, There's a Way!

You must first *really want* whatever it is that you're trying to sustain and then resolve that you'll do whatever it takes to make it work. Willpower is merely a willingness to do what it takes, while closing the back door on any escape plan.

In the meantime, you may have to find other jobs to make ends meet. You may have to sell your big house to make it easier financially to start your dream business (you may even have to sell your big house ten years after starting your dream business in order to continue building your dream). Only you know if you're willing to sacrifice the "means" to get to the end. Are you willing to trade in immediate gratification for long-term success?

Some people can't—they simply won't "do" now to enjoy the payoff later. They won't put in the schooling to become the doctor or veterinarian they'd always planned on being. They won't sacrifice the parties, socializing, and good times to get their deadlines met. They won't do the inner work required to deal with the "stuff" that's been stopping them from settling down and raising the family they say they want most. These are the same people who complain 20 years later when they're no further ahead, when they have bodies that are falling apart because of years of abuse.

Are you willing to do what it takes to sustain success?

The 10,000-Hour Rule

The best way to develop staying power is through practice, practice, practice!

Keep doing what you're doing until you get so comfortable, so good, so confident, so sure that you know "you know" . . . and it no longer feels like effort. You may even feel like you've lost some of the excitement—that's a great sign that you're creating a habit! The first time you brushed your *own* teeth, cut the grass, washed the dishes, or did your laundry, it was exciting, too! Excitement doesn't equate to success. Passion may be what lights you up, but having massive amounts of passion is still not enough to sustain success. You must practice your skills until they become second nature—until they become a part of you.

Malcolm Gladwell's book *The Outliers* draws on story after story, example after brilliant example, of some of the most successful people known. They had all put exorbitant amounts of time into their trade. From the world's best hockey players to the Beatles, Bill Gates, and even Mozart—they all followed what Gladwell calls "The 10,000-Hour Rule." "Practice isn't the thing you do once you're good," Gladwell says. "It's the thing you do that makes you good."

Are you willing to put in 10,000 hours before you decide to move onto a new dream . . . 10,000 hours before you are even considered an expert? That many hours works out to 250 weeks, at 40 hours a week. Since there are 52 weeks in a year—that's nearly five years to just get good at your trade, if you did it 40 hours a week! At 20 hours a week, that's 10 years. At 10 hours a week to practice, that's nearly 20 years! How many hours a week do you put into your passion? Are you willing to put in the time to perfect your skills and sustain success?

If not, you don't really want it or just aren't willing to do what it takes! Sorry to burst your bubble, but nothing comes without the effort required, whether a great relationship with your mate, children, God, dogs, or money. Now you understand the saying: "Time is your most precious commodity."

I Know—It's Hard!

If you talked to most highly successful people, they would tell you that it took hard work, perseverance, focus, and the right plan. I bet they'd also tell you that they had a little bit of good luck thrown in from time to time. Even so, there were many times when they felt like giving up (*and nearly did*), but something always brought them back. I'll bet there were times they felt like frauds or felt inadequate, ill-equipped, and even terrified . . . but something always told them to stay the course.

When Failure Isn't an Option, You'll Succeed

The inspiring story of Thomas Edison and his 10,000 attempts to create the lightbulb should give us the encouragement to never give up. *Yes, that's right!* Edison tried more than 10,000 different ways to make a glass bulb light up, and at least 9,999 times were failures. I bet it was hard for him. I bet there were moments of frustration, hair pulling, and even the odd time he felt like throwing in the towel. But he never did. I'm sure he had to continually rework his plan and stay focused on his dream of putting electric lights into homes around the world. Something in him believed that he could do it.

Don't ever assume it was easy—not for Thomas Edison, Abraham Lincoln, Mahatma Gandhi, Mother Teresa, Babe Ruth, Amelia Earhart, Susan B. Anthony, Joan of Arc, Martin Luther King, Jr., Oprah Winfrey, Barack Obama . . . or even for your own parents! There are millions of empowered people who have blessed our world by stepping into their power—we just don't know their names. Whether your aspiration is to do something on a global, national, or regional scale, or on a level in your own backyard, your dreams matter . . . and manifesting those dreams takes effort. Don't ever kid yourself!

What I remind myself of is that it takes more drudgery to get up every day and go to a job you hate. It takes more exertion to live in an overweight body, dependent on medication. I know firsthand that it's downright draining to be in an unfulfilling relationship or to be around someone who is negative or condescending. To me, that's far harder than the energy required to keep the faith, believe in your dream, and take action! Nobody ever said it was going to be easy . . . but what's the alternative?

Are you ready to stop waiting for someone . . . *anyone* . . . to wake up and notice you—notice your talents, needs, wants, and desires? Are you ready to accept yourself for who you are (for all your supposed faults, weaknesses, addictions, fears, syndromes, and dysfunctions) and love yourself regardless? If so, you are ready to become an empowered person! You're ready to begin creating a magnificent life!

I'm sure you've given yourself too many "outs" in the past, too many permissible excuses, but they just don't cut it anymore. You have a choice: to keep doing what you've been doing or to do something you've never done before. Sure, this may scare you and maybe you're not exactly sure what to do yet. You'll find out. You'll make the calls, do the research, and discover your next steps. You don't have to know the whole journey today; you just need to begin moving in the right direction.

Remind yourself that you're worth more than you've been. Your life is worth more than you've been living. Don't beat yourself up, guilt yourself, or blame others for your situation. *It is what it is,* and you've learned so much along the way. You're not going to wait for anyone to give you permission to be *you.* You're not going to wait anymore for someone to come along and give you the money you need to start that business, set you up on that blind date, or fix your dysfunctional family. You're taking charge. You're going to treat yourself the way you want to be treated and stop resisting yourself and your dreams. You'll no longer resist asking for help when you need it or doing the things that may feel a little uncomfortable.

From this day forward, assume complete accountability for your life. You must take charge of it and do what you need to do to create a life that is genuinely yours: a life that has purpose, meaning, joy, and value. You will no longer rob yourself of your dignity, integrity, and self-respect by blaming, waiting, hoping, and praying that someone will show up and give you the things you want. You know that "if it's going to be, it's up to me."

You know that to achieve an empowered life, you must reach higher. You must step out of your comfort zone and your need to seek permission to live your greatest life. Make a list each evening, just before going to bed, of the seven essential action steps you need to take the next day—seven steps that will bring you closer to your goals. Start each morning with the most important step.

You are the master of your destiny, the captain of your ship. Every choice you make (or don't make) is yours. *Never give up!*

Afterword

THE LAST KEY
TO SUCCESS...

❖ ❖ ❖

*T*here's one last subject I've barely touched on, yet it's one of the most vital keys for creating and sustaining success. This simple but magical ingredient is available to absolutely everyone—no matter what your situation, who you are, where you live, how old or young you are, or how much money you have. I can't overstate the importance of this last key. . . .

It's not until you completely open your heart and experience genuine gratitude that you will shift into a realm of consciousness that's not easily accessible to the average, wary person. Genuine gratitude not only unlocks your spirit, but it also connects you to a universal spirit, which I call the Divine Universal Collective Energy, or DUCE. It is an infinite intelligence, the place where your sixth sense connects. Gratitude shifts your resonance to a channel that receives this divine frequency where ideas and visions come to you, and insights and peace wash over you.

When I feel the presence of the DUCE, my legs actually "hum" and occasionally my ears will ring. I know that whatever

I'm working on is something very powerful! I smile and give thanks for being a conduit of consciousness. My good friend, the extremely talented musician Natalie Hughes, says that when she's performing her best work, she feels like she enters a whole new level where she doesn't even feel like she's the one who is singing! *That's tapped in!*

The best way for me to evoke this energy is to enter into a quiet space of pureness, of total reverence and complete presence. It's a place within where I breathe and say, "Ah . . . thank you. I am so blessed. I am so grateful for all I have." Then I remain there until every cell of my being feels it, too. Often it comes simply from repeating the words *thank you* over and over.

This key to lasting empowerment is to become awestruck for what you already have, knowing that no matter what happens, you'll be okay! Desire may be the root of all achievement, but it's only through genuine gratitude that achievement can be realized. Until this moment arrives, you'll continually want for more, never satisfying the hunger of desire.

Become grateful for everything even if you think there isn't a lot to love in your life. Think of the one thing that always makes you feel sincerely thankful and appreciative: a steaming cup of your favorite coffee, a warm bed on a cold night, a roof over your head (even one that leaks), or a half-full refrigerator of food (it could be empty!). The more you give thanks, the more you'll recognize the incredible amount of blessings already in your life. The key is *genuine* gratitude. Being nice is one thing, but pretending to love the things you don't is inauthentic.

The final question to ask yourself is: *How can I love <u>more</u> things in my life?* Then find a way to do that very thing—*love more!* Each evening, just after you make a list of your action steps, write down as many things as you can that make you feel thankful. What a beautiful sleep you'll have! What an open conduit you'll be as you drift off to sleep. . . .

❖ ❖ ❖

As this book comes to a close, I leave you with one last thought: *Create your greatest life!* Not to show off your worth or prove yourself to anyone, but because it's what you want. Remember that God only wants for you what you want. God is within you and you are within God. Glory be! Why wouldn't he want *only* greatness for you?

Once you realize just how magnificent and important you are (*which you are!*), you'll want to start creating. You'll know without doubt that it's your God-given destiny, your birthright. When you embrace this, you will intuitively know exactly what to create and, even easier, how to sustain it.

From one light worker to another: *The world is counting on you. Shine bright!*

ACKNOWLEDGMENTS

❖ ❖ ❖

I never thought it was possible to write a book in less than a month while also working on a TV show; running my own business; raising three children; helping my five-pound Maltese dog give birth (a middle of the night emergency C-section that left one puppy dead and one alive—and yes, we're keeping our little "Miracle"!); taking in a 16-year-old boy who was living in a garage; throwing my father's 60th birthday party at my home; spending time with my husband; doing a 9-day cellular cleanse; running 5k each morning; and then racing off to give a talk in Aruba . . . but that's exactly what happened! Love really does move mountains, and I loved writing this book. *Loving something is a good sign that you're on the right track!*

I'm indebted to my wonderful friend and Customer Care Specialist at Crystal Andrus Productions, Helen Valenzuela, who knocked off chapters at a time, proofreading and correcting my grammar like an English teacher would (she did teach French, Spanish, and Latin, along with special education, for over 30 years). Helen, you gave me such strength and confidence. I can't thank you enough! You are a special soul.

I want to thank my beautiful children, Madelaine and Julia, who have listened endlessly as I "talk the talk," and I pray that as you both venture out into life, you will "walk the walk." I especially need to thank Edson, my young brother, who sat many evenings strumming his guitar while I read him page after page. I'm not sure if you were too polite to leave or if you really enjoyed it, but I loved having you listen.

Thank you to my amazing Dream Team of SWAT coaches, especially Nicole McCance, Adele Fridman, Shannon Doran, and Helen Valenzuela.

Thank you to my partners (and dear friends) at the SWAT Institute, Annette Doose and Wendy Cowles. You've helped me manifest a lifelong dream. I am indebted to you both.

Thank you to my SWAT Ambassadors who share the gift of empowerment with women around the globe—you are incredible light workers!

Thank you to Rae Wittenberg! My little "Rae" of sunshine, you make coming to work each and every day fun! Shine bright!

A huge and heartfelt thank-you to Natalie Hughes. You have the voice, heart, talent, and spirit of an angel. I am honored to work with you and to call you my dear, *dear* friend.

Thank you to Jill Kramer, the editorial director at Hay House who runs her "house" like a loving and devoted mother; Shannon Littrell, who has a special touch and amazing patience; Lisa Mitchell, my personal editor who paid attention to detail like no other and whose support of this book meant so much to me; Amy Rose Grigoriou, who designed the fantastic cover; Charles McStravick, who created the amazing book design; along with the entire team at Hay House. And finally, Reid Tracy and Louise Hay—my Earth angels! *Thank you, thank you, thank you!*

Thank you to Korby Banner, photographer extraordinaire, for the great cover photo and fabulous beauty tips, along with years of support and friendship. Thank you to Kamen Nikolov, for seven years of devoted talent—thank you for helping create my brand identity. You're an intricate part of my success. Blessings to you and your family! And to Peggy Murrah's brilliant team—Mandy Bobolia, Patty Dost, and Kathy Colaiacovo. You're the most dynamic group of women, and I'm so blessed to work with you!

Last, I want to thank my husband, Aaron Morissette—my light protector and partner in life, love, and business. Sometimes these three small words just aren't enough, but truly . . . *I love you.*

ABOUT THE AUTHOR

❖ ❖ ❖

Crystal Andrus is a worldwide leader in the field of self-discovery and personal transformation. From a tough beginning—sexual abuse, moving out at 15, battling health scares, huge weight gain, a difficult divorce, and near bankruptcy before becoming a single mother of two daughters—she has risen to become a best-selling author, motivational speaker, women's advocate, nutritionist, and the weight-loss expert on the international hit TV show *X-Weighted,* seen in more than 15 countries. Her first book, *Simply . . . Woman!* was a blockbuster in 2006, coming in at #14 as the Reader's Choice at Chapters, Indigo, and Coles across Canada.

A personal coach to people from all walks of life—including celebrities, medical doctors, artists, musicians, scientists, psychologists, and other best-selling authors and coaches, as well as regular people in need—Crystal's passion is to help those who are ready and willing to become the heroes of their own lives.

Touring with The Power Within and I Can Do It® Hay House events has allowed Crystal to share the stage with some of today's most influential people, including Sir Richard Branson, Dr. Phil, Louise Hay, Dr. Wayne Dyer, Suze Orman, Dr. Christiane Northrup, and many others.

Certified by the American College of Sports Medicine and Canadian School of Natural Nutrition, she is the CEO and founder of Crystal Andrus Productions, which is dedicated to creating health and healing products, CDs, DVDs, retreats, and telecourses. Crystal is also the founder of the SWAT Institute (Simply Woman Accredited Training), an online Empowerment Coaching school.

Crystal lives in a grand old farmhouse in a tiny town in southern Ontario with her husband, children, four dogs, cats, a hamster, and a flock of singing canaries.

Please visit Crystal at **www.crystalandrus.com** and **www.SWATInstitute.com.**

We hope you enjoyed this Hay House book.
If you'd like to receive our online catalog featuring additional
information on Hay House books and products, or if you'd like to
find out more about the Hay Foundation, please contact:

Hay House, Inc., P.O. Box 5100, Carlsbad, CA 92018-5100

(760) 431-7695 or (800) 654-5126
(760) 431-6948 (fax) or (800) 650-5115 (fax)
www.hayhouse.com® • www.hayfoundation.org

❖ ❖ ❖

Published and distributed in Australia by:
Hay House Australia Pty. Ltd., 18/36 Ralph St., Alexandria NSW 2015
Phone: 612-9669-4299 • *Fax:* 612-9669-4144
www.hayhouse.com.au

Published and distributed in the United Kingdom by:
Hay House UK, Ltd., 292B Kensal Rd., London W10 5BE • *Phone:*
44-20-8962-1230 • *Fax:* 44-20-8962-1239 • www.hayhouse.co.uk

Published and distributed in the Republic of South Africa by:
Hay House SA (Pty), Ltd., P.O. Box 990, Witkoppen 2068 • *Phone/*
Fax: 27-11-467-8904 • info@hayhouse.co.za • www.hayhouse.co.za

Published in India by:
Hay House Publishers India, Muskaan Complex, Plot No. 3, B-2,
Vasant Kunj, New Delhi 110 070 • *Phone:* 91-11-4176-1620
Fax: 91-11-4176-1630 • www.hayhouse.co.in

Distributed in Canada by:
Raincoast, 9050 Shaughnessy St., Vancouver, B.C. V6P 6E5
Phone: (604) 323-7100 • *Fax:* (604) 323-2600 • www.raincoast.com

❖ ❖ ❖

Take Your Soul on a Vacation

Visit **www.HealYourLife.com®** to regroup, recharge, and reconnect
with your own magnificence. Featuring blogs, mind-body-spirit
news, and life-changing wisdom from Louise Hay and friends.

Visit **www.HealYourLife.com** today!